DAVID ADJAYE

MAKING PUBLIC BUILDINGS

SPECIFICITY CUSTOMIZATION IMBRICATION

Edited by Peter Allison

Thames & Hudson

Contents

Preface

One of Britain's leading contemporary architects, David Adjaye combines the sensual and emotive with a conceptual approach to the fundamental elements of architecture. Refusing to reduce his formal vocabulary to a signature style, he has instead explored scale, measurement, space, light and materials in projects that have included private homes, retail spaces and public buildings. While attention has been focused mainly on his domestic projects, this publication focuses on Adjaye's projects in the public realm.

Since setting up his own practice in 1994, Adjaye's buildings have emphasised the experience as much as the functionality of the built environment: 'Buildings are deeply emotive structures which form our psyche. People think they're just things they manoeuvre through. But the make-up of a person is influenced by the nature of spaces'. Adjaye's greatest concern is to make space itself present, to intensify its experience through almost sculpted shafts of light, different tonalities of colour and materials that reflect and absorb and that combine the smooth with the rough, the refined with the ready made. He choreographs his materials into spaces that do not reveal themselves immediately, eliciting instead a series of physical reactions as the buildings unfold. His process and approach fuse the architectural with the artistic, and has resulted in a number of collaborations with artists such as Olafur Eliasson and Chris Ofili. These have often taken the form of temporary pavilions, transitory moments of contemplation and reflection that interrupt our daily experience of public space.

In many ways, Adjaye's buildings rise from within. In his interview with Peter Allison published here, Adjaye speaks of his public buildings as public rooms, marked by an informality 'that is about everyday reality'. His attention to material is one of the elements that he deploys to this effect. It invites a sensory and phenomenal encounter that evokes early Modernist architecture while rejecting its cold austerity, and provokes what

he has described elsewhere as 'a little hallucinogenic moment when the visitor is deceived into thinking a building is not an institution'. Yet his public buildings also find their place in the surrounding topography, by rising and falling to meet their neighbours or, like his Stephen Lawrence Centre in Deptford, London, opening up and dividing into two to give access to the river beyond. Others, like the Whitechapel Idea Store, overhang onto the busy pavement below. An escalator rises up from the street, as though accommodating the street's rhythms by swiftly conveying users inside. Its patterned glass skin echoes the canopies on the market stalls in front while opening up the library, traditionally a sealed chamber, to the cityscape outside.

David Adjaye's recent engagement with public buildings comes at a time of renewed urgency and debate around notions of publicness. His designs have so far engaged with the different definitions that museums, pavilions, libraries, learning centres and social housing propose. In his essay for this publication, Okwui Enwezor locates Adjaye's significance within a concept of democracy that allows for multiple and contrasting voices: 'Adjaye begins his buildings precisely with the idea that a civil concord must exist between users, yet with a maximum potential for the exercise of difference rather than social conformity.' He points in particular to buildings such as the Bernie Grant Centre in Tottenham, London, or the Nobel Peace Center, Oslo, that embody the social and political tensions of the present rather than a bland notion of inclusivity; he finds in Adjaye's two Idea Stores an archive born of 'a whole complex of production between the community and the local government', physically addressed through the buildings' direct engagement with the pavement. Saskia Sassen equally frames Adjaye's practice within a shift from 'civic to politicised urban space', marked by 'fragmentations along multiple differences'. She begins by considering the monumentality and functionalism of current urban developments, contrasting these to the modest scale of Adjaye's buildings. Sassen argues that this modesty is in part defined by an emphasis on making that constitutes publicness as a process of negotiation. She sees the walls in Adjaye's buildings as a 'third space' rather than a dividing line; a space that activates a dialogue through an emphasis on sensory engagement. Sassen also proposes that the simultaneity of Adjaye's buildings can begin to 'reinvent and reposition' more fluid notions of the local.

Nikolaus Hirsch situates discussions around publicness within the relationship between form and function. He argues that, in a period in which institutions present 'paradigms of extreme environmental control', one of the avenues open to the architect in considering a more 'porous' relationship to community is the choice and application of material. He finds in Adjaye's sense of materiality 'opportunism, superficiality, ruse, narration and appropriation', elements that suggest publicness without prescribing its parameters. Peter Allison continues this argument by exploring the formal properties of Adjaye's buildings and their relationship to each building's physical surroundings. He begins with a discussion of Adjaye's 2004 pavilion *LxWxH*, a rectangular tube that in many ways acts as the architect's basic unit, to highlight the ways in which Adjaye derives the spatial relations of his structures from the dimensions of their sites, while materials such as glass and timber allow for a continuing dialogue between interior and exterior.

Also included here are two interviews with the architect, which provide an in-depth analysis of his own work. The first, with Peter Allison, speaks from his practice and provides a revealing insight into Adjaye's method and approach to materiality, form, function, site and notions of public space. Their conversation also extends to consider some of Adjaye's influences and the significance of his collaborative projects. Kodwo Eshun, on the other hand, joins Adjaye on a tour of Africa, India and South America, to consider multiple notions of public space. As a whole, they reveal an architect intent on a contemporary engagement with the western modernist canon, re-inventing it anew with lessons learned from a plurality of simultaneous global models.

ANDREA TARSIA
Head of Exhibitions and Projects, Whitechapel Gallery

This publication accompanies *Making Public Buildings*, David Adjaye's exhibition at the Whitechapel Gallery, London. We are delighted that the Netherlands Architecture Institute Maastricht, The Studio Museum in Harlem, New York, the Museum of Contemporary Art, Denver and the Arario Gallery, Beijing have all agreed to collaborate on Adjaye's first major exhibition, bringing his practice to further international attention.

We would like to thank the following, whose generosity has helped bring this ambitious project to fruition: The Graham Foundation, Francesca von Habsburg, founder of Thyssen-Bornemisza Art Contemporary, the Royal Commission for the Exhibition of 1851, Davis Langdon, John Eldridge, SJ Berwin LLP, and Matthew Slotover and Amanda Sharp, Frieze Art Fair; as well as Icon, Media Partner for the exhibition.

This publication is in collaboration with Thames & Hudson, and we would like to thank Lucas Dietrich for lending his expertise. Peter Allison has worked closely with the architect in giving shape to the contents of this book, while Okwui Enwezor, Kodwo Eshun, Nikolaus Hirsch and Saskia Sassen have provided revealing insights into Adjaye's practice. Our heartfelt thanks go especially to Karen Wong, Hannah Booth, James Branch, Rashid Ali along with everyone at Adjaye/Associates for their energy, commitment and vision; and to David Adjaye, for effortlessly translating his complex and extraordinary buildings into the modest confines of an exhibition.

IWONA BLAZWICK
Director, Whitechapel Gallery

POPULAR SOVEREIGNTY AND PUBLIC SPACE: DAVID ADJAYE'S ARCHITECTURE OF IMMANENCE

OKWUI ENWEZOR

PUBLIC SPACE AND CIVIL SOCIETY

A couple of years ago I published an essay on the work and activities of Le Groupe Amos and Huit Facettes, two activist/intellectual/artist groups operating in the Democratic Republic of Congo and Senegal respectively.[1] The countries which are the base of their operations, in which they produce their work, are broadly speaking different in their political formations. The Democratic Republic of Congo (DRC), often described as a failed state, is ruled by an autocratic regime, despite the democratic appellation in its name. Senegal is nominally a democracy, in the sense that elections occur there at twenty-year intervals. That said, I was interested in how Le Groupe Amos and Huit Facettes conceive their operations and practices around notions of public and social space. Most importantly, I wanted to understand how their respective practices pointed towards the generation, through the formalisation of discursive symbols, of a network of relations between urban and rural citizens living in each country. The central motif of the groups' efforts was predicated on social interaction and contact between a range of political and economic classes, agents and actors, ethnic and gender groups coming together as participants in a cultural and political conversation. This conversation is often organised around the symbolic frame of art and representation. There is always an active mise-en-scene through which the participants make their contributions. In the DRC for example, Le Groupe Amos has worked on surpassing and piercing the dichotomy inherent in the urban context of Kinshasa, where citizens exist between two zones: La Ville (the urban district) and La Cité (the suburban).[2] In Senegal, Huit Facettes seeks to bridge the gap between the city and the village.

In Kinshasa this separation has led to spatial and temporal atomisation between the urban and suburban. This is further exacerbated by the fact that La Ville represents the heart of official culture and its symbols of political and economic power. While La Cité is a space of negativity (crime, poverty, hunger, death) and made all the more impoverished by its lack of access to power and resources. The less privileged zones, where the workers, labourers, domestic workers, petty traders, and assorted inhabitants live, exist on the rim of official amnesia. This dichotomy between La Ville (the official centre) and La Cité (the outlying neighbourhoods), constitutes two competing impressions of public space. And where democratic norms are absent it forces a different kind of disclosure, namely the fact that public space as such is never a given in all contexts. To develop a proper praxis and theory of public space requires us to acknowledge this basic fact. According to Rosalyn Deutsche 'How we define public space is intimately connected with ideas about what it means to be human, the nature of society, and the kind of political community we want.'[3] For a city such as Kinshasa, which exists under constant threat of political anarchy, Deutsche's point is absolutely paramount. All the more so, because it is the networks between society and the political community, and the inhabitants who form other communities, that remain the most fragile and in need of the most renovation. In this sense, it is not public space but civil society towards which one must first direct attention. It is these shifting impressions that animate the critical work of Le Groupe Amos and Huit Facettes respectively. Within each of their operations, it is immediately noticeable that public space is never a given. It must constantly be produced but as a fundamental part of civil society. This point is adumbrated in each of their praxis. Through their interdisciplinary and transnational networks they posit the transformation of the artwork into an immaterial symbol of social dialogue. Thereby turning their work into the production of social space[4] and community in the given ethical/political realignments that were becoming visible in the two countries.

BETWEEN FREE AND EQUAL CITIZENS

I begin with these two groups, because their interdisciplinary work bears on what I see as the major task confronting all architects who are planning buildings that come, *a priori*, with the designation: public space. In little less than a decade, David Adjaye's work has become increasingly located in what I would call the intermediary zone between public space and civil society. In the 'state of exception'[5] that characterises the current global context, one which is rife with shifting political allegiances, economic restructuring, the rise of conflict between ethnic and religious communities,[6] immigration, terrorism, and other contestations, it has become clear that public space is now under suspension. Even if it were the case that such an entity exists, it would still require a clear rethinking of its definition along with an expanded understanding of civil society.

But in order to address the issue of what we can make of public space in this stage of a late capitalist and resurgent neo-liberal framework, in this time of assault on democratic norms, enactment of emergency powers, and suspension of entente cordiale, we may need to ask: Is public space what we mean when we encounter the decadent spaces of bourgeois culture in the innumerable repressive plazas, miniature parks, shopping malls, promenades, museums, etc. which today, define the instrumental logic of global economic conditions controlled by private industry and speculative capitalism? Or is it the ostentatious and pretentious *tchotchke* of autocratic and dictatorial power that sublimates public

memory in the figure of the ruler? Who can forget the staged toppling of Saddam Hussein's statue from its pedestal in Firdos Square in Baghdad in the Spring of 2003, a toppling reminiscent of the assault by partisan revolutionaries on the Czar's statue in Eisenstein's 1927 film *October*. It is increasingly obvious to all that even under the best democratic conditions, there is no ontological public space as such. Rather public space, which is often understood as the *sine qua non* of all democratic and open societies, may in fact exist purely as a legal phantasm. Public space is never an open space. It is constantly legislated, monitored, and reconnoitered by official institutions. Adjaye himself recognises some of these contradictions and insists that as an architect, there is no *fait accompli* in the idea of public space.[7]

For Adjaye public space is always contingent, always in the process of realisation. We do not build public space; we construct it through a variety of individual governmentalities. Therefore it is not so much the institution or buildings designated as such, rather it is the silent but obvious amenities (recognised by everyday users as symbols of the publicness of space) that he as an architect must constantly make visible for any aspect of his architecture to acquire the quality of public space. In this sense, public space is not a thing but a value-added quality to an already existing structure. As an architect this pushes Adjaye towards elaborating within his buildings a 'third space', a kind of illusionary and concrete zone[8] of maximum interaction and social discourse between publics, individuals, communities, experts, and non-experts. This is essentially a conception of democratic space, one predicated both on the intelligibility of design and the distinctiveness of function, use, ethic, and value. In a fundamental way, Adjaye begins his buildings precisely with the idea that a civil concord must exist between users, yet with a maximum potential for the exercise of difference rather than social conformity.

Chantal Mouffe makes precisely the same point with regards to participatory democracy in her theory of an 'agonistic model of democracy' that is based on a principle of deliberation 'between free and equal citizens'.[9] This interaction comes with the supposition that there is exchange in the encounters and negotiations that happen between free and equal citizens. It is a representation of social recognition. Fundamentally, the issue of recognition hinges on the Habermasian notion of popular sovereignty.[10] Public space, then, is not a designated place overseen by corporate interest for maximum tax rebate, or as part of the fiction of good corporate citizenship that is financed by the state. It is rather an active space for the expression of popular sovereignty, an agonistic public sphere.[11] For Mouffe, who is critical of what she calls a politics of consensus that has abolished the distinction between the ideological self-understanding of the left and right, the agonistic public sphere is not the end of an adversarial politics of recognition, but its beginning. She goes on to define her terms for agonism: she states that 'in democratic societies, while conflict cannot and should not be eradicated, neither should it take the form of a struggle between enemies (antagonism), but rather between adversaries (agonism).'[12]

THE MUSEUM AND THE MEMORIAL

So far, we have concentrated on the non-utilitarian/ functionalist approach to the architectural use of the discourse of public space, to address my worry about the potential complicity of architecture in maintaining a border between popular sovereignty and the forms of social and ideological prestige that accompany many commissions. Museum architecture exemplifies this more than any other type of public building today: it represents the conjunction of forms of spectacle, capitalism and political populism. The new Museum of Modern Art in New York is a recent example of this type of architecture. In both its programme and architecture, MoMA has unabashedly and without apology collapsed forms of spectacle and populism. But we must ask whether it is possible to continue with the pretence that museums are socially viable public spaces, when the public that attends its functions are seen as little more than characters in a circus of organized high cultural delirium. Museums of art are often described in terms of their 'public' mission. And the artworks they hold in terms of 'public' trust. Under the prevailing conditions of neo-liberalism and the iron rule of capitalism, in whose vital interest is the 'public' museum? This question bears substantially on the function and role of the museum today, especially in light of the crisis in the global public sphere and of the fact that since its inception the museum as a public institution has been governed by the private interest of a bourgeois elite.

Adjaye is more than aware of this vexing issue, especially, given the shimmering high aesthetics of his building designs. It would be a pity if the elegant libraries, museums, education centres which he has been designing of late were to be understood purely from the view point of their middle-brow aspiration and high cultural obfuscation. It has been fortuitous for Adjaye that some of the buildings he has been designing are of such social and political character that they have given him a free lease to both build institutions and challenge their various orthodoxies. In fact, the buildings have provided the testing ground to elaborate on the questions that have impeded the creation of agonistic public spaces so far. Consequently, Adjaye is designing some of his best architecture around contestations that illuminate the fractured civil society in Great Britain today. It could be said that the commissions in London for the Stephen Lawrence Centre, Deptford, Bernie Grant Arts Centre, Tottenham, Idea Store, Chrisp Street and Whitechapel, both in the East End, are being undertaken in the shadow of Lord Tebbitt's politics of antagonism and disrecognition of a viable multicultural Britain. Similarly, the Nobel Peace Center, Oslo, comes at a time when international civil society is beleaguered. The Stephen Lawrence Centre, Bernie Grant Arts Centre, and Nobel Peace Center have been carefully designed around the commemorative functions of the memorial and the monument; particularly, in light of the role that each of the individuals commemorated and that the Nobel Institute's position play in reminding each of us about our roles, responsibilities, and rights as citizens.

Each of these buildings are located in the fault lines of political turmoil and a broadening social struggle — the Stephen Lawrence Centre is a great flashpoint that commemorates a black victim of police brutality and racism, the Bernie Grant Arts Centre honours a pioneering black British political figure, and the Nobel Peace Center is dedicated to social justice. Designing such buildings is as rare as it is daunting for an architect who is still in his thirties to undertake all at once. This makes Adjaye not simply an architect/designer but equally an intellectual broker between the most complex issues of our time, moderating between ethics and politics, public space and civil society, popular sovereignty and public sphere, La Ville and La Cité.

THE ARCHIVE AND THE SIDEWALK
The Idea Store is essentially a local library, a centre of learning, research and exchange; a market place for ideas, a contact zone of knowledge. It is worth considering the associations the notion of a store evokes. In the immediate, elemental sense it calls up images of a trading house in the community, the corner store, the neighbourhood's provision shop. The provision shop provides the goods for sustenance of the body. Like wise, the Idea Store embodies the same kind of opportunity to feed that deep hunger for self-determination and self-enlightenment. The notion of store also suggests a kind of repository, where things are kept, placed in reserve, stored for preservation, archived: a site of commencement and commandment.[13] Thinking of the Idea Store in

this way opens up its archontic imperative, that is to say, its conception not only as a library but as an archive. But this archive is not singular. It is part of a whole complex of production between the community and the local government, each of which generates, as it interacts with the archive, its own interpretative decisions. Derrida has written that 'a science of the archive must include the theory of this institutionalisation, that is to say, the theory both of the law which begins by inscribing itself there and of the right which authorises it'.[14]

A science of the archive equally correlates with that sense of place which Henri Lefebvre calls social space. It is a place of multiplicity: a meeting space indivisible from the diverse urban identities that inhabit it, that binds together a contemporary city's multi-ethnic, multicultural communities and memories. According to Lefebvre '(Social) space is not a thing among other things, nor a product among other products: rather it subsumes things produced, and encompasses their interrelationships in their coexistence and simultaneity... Itself the outcome of past actions, social space is what permits fresh actions to occur ... Social space implies a great diversity of knowledge.'[15] Inasmuch as the Idea Store represents and reproduces the function of a communal space, Adjaye has employed Lefebvre's concept to outline the social value of this architecture by integrating and folding the structures into the skin of the regular commercial activities of the street: lined with shops, vendors, food stalls, mosques, churches, etc. It is literally a horizontal plane. It needs emphasising here, the importance of the sidewalk in this jostle and bustle that defines the life of the street. In a subtle way the archive is now conjoined with the street. It is part of the daily trading that occurs there. We may not have noticed this intersection, because the sidewalk is perhaps the most anomalous and unremarked of spaces in the social interaction that defines relationships on the street.

The luminous intelligence of Adjaye's design is to point us towards that recognition, but in the least ostentatious and propagandistic manner. It is here that the threshold of the Idea Store lies. The sidewalk represents the welcome mat into the Idea Store, which is not inseparable from the street. Perhaps one can suggest that the obsolescence of corporate architecture and the so-called public plazas that surround it, is derived from its lack of interaction with the liminal dimension of the sidewalk, which is fundamentally a democratic space. Architects should do more to recognise the powerful incentive for the production of public space which the sidewalk offers. Artists such as Liisa Roberts with her public sculpture *Sidewalk*, 1999 recognized this. Richard Serra with *Tilted Arc*, 1981 did not and hence became a victim of his own impoverished understanding of public space, which is not a place, but a space of negotiation and encounter between free and equal citizens. Can it be possible to say then — in this time of terror and emergency rule — that the sidewalk represents a fundamental part of the new architecture of the democratic public sphere.[16] And how much can Adjaye's architectural projects absorb their potential in order to supply those amenities that lead towards the production of public space?

Notes

1. See Okwui Enwezor, *The Production of Social Space as Artwork: Protocols of Community in the Work of Le Groupe Amos and Huit Facettes in A Fiction of Authenticity: Contemporary Africa Abroad*, Shannon Fitzgerald and Tumelo Mosaka, editors (St. Louis: Contemporary Art Museum, 2003) p. 53–68

2. See Thierry Nlandu, *Kinshasa: Beyond Chaos in Under Seige: Four African Cities, Freetown, Johannesburg, Kinshasa, Lagos, Documenta11_Platform 4*, editors, Okwui Enwezor, Carlos Basualdo, Ute Meta Bauer, Sussane Ghez, Sarat Maharaj, Mark Nash, Octavio Zaya (Stuttgart: Hatje Cantz, 2002) p. 185–199

3. Rosalyn Deutsche, *Evictions: Art and Spatial Politics* (Cambridge, MA: MIT Press, 1996) p. 269

4. See Henri Lefebvre, *The Production of Space*, translator, Donald Nicholson-Smith (Oxford and Malden, MA: Blackwell Publishing, 1991)

5. See Giorgio Agamben, *State of Exception*, translator, Kevin Attel (Chicago: University of Chicago Press, 2005)

6. This conflict exemplifies the disorder in Europe today, beginning with the bombings in Madrid and London, the defeat of the European constitution in Holland and France, and the riots that have riven the Banlieu (those functionalist ghettos) in France to mention just a few.

7. Telephone conversation between Adjaye and the author, November 23, 2005.

8. See Edward Soja, *Third Space: Journeys to Los Angeles and Other Real-and-Imagined Places* (Oxford and Malden, MA: Blackwell, 1996)

9. Chantal Mouffe, *The Democratic Paradox* (London and New York: Verso, 2000) p.80–107 Mouffe, p. 85

10. Mouffe p. 85

11. See Mouffe, *For an Agonistic Public Sphere in Democracy Unrealized: Documenta11_Platform 1*, editors, Okwui Enwezor, Carlos Basualdo, Ute Meta Bauer, Sussane Ghez, Sarat Maharaj, Mark Nash, Octavio Zaya (Stuttgart: Hatje Cantz, 2002)

12. Ibid. p. 90

13. Jacques Derrida, *Archive Fever: A Freudian Impression*, translator, Eric Prenowitz (Chicago: University of Chicago Press, 1996)

14. Ibid. p. 4

15. Henri Lefebvre, *The Production of Space*, translator, Donald Nicholson-Smith (Oxford and Malden, MA: Blackwell Publishing, 1991) p. 73

16. See Jurgen Habermas, *The Structural Transformation of the Public Sphere*, translator, Thomas Burger with Frederick Lawrence (Cambridge: Polity Press, 1989)

BUILT COMPLEXITY AND PUBLIC ENGAGEMENTS

SASKIA SASSEN

The enormity of urban development, the overwhelming presence of massive architectures and dense infra-structures, the irresistible utility logics that organise much investment in cities, all have produced displacement and estrangement among many individuals and whole communities. These conditions unsettle older notions and experiences of public space. While the monumentalised public spaces of European cities remain vibrant sites for various rituals and routines, the overall trend is a shift from a participatory architecture to an architecture of demonstration and display. David Adjaye's projects ask us to think about an architecture for modest public spaces in today's city, aimed at recovering the possibility of making publicness.

Today's city is not a monolith. It contains multiple under-used spaces, often marked more by memory than by current meaning. These spaces are part of the interiority of a city yet lie outside its organising, utility-driven logics and spatial frames. They are *terrain vagues*[1] that allow many residents to find niches within the architecture of demonstration. Subjectively, connecting to such *terrains vagues* allows one to bypass the massive structures that have increasingly come to dominate. But the *terrain vague* pulls individuals into their heads and away from the experience of public space.

And yet, there is a type of urban condition that dwells between the fact of massive structures and the reality of under-used spaces. I think it is central to the experience of the urban, and it makes legible transitions and unsettlements inherent in this experience. It can also reinsert the possibility of making — *poesis* — in a way that massive projects do not. The making I am interested in here is of modest public spaces, constituted

through the practices of people and critical archi-tectural interventions that are on small or medium level scales. These are not monumentalised public spaces nor are they marked by large-scale structures. They open up a question about the current urban condition in ways that take us beyond today's engagements with high-tech architecture, virtual spaces, simulacra, theme parks. All of the latter matter, but they are fragments of an incomplete puzzle.

The work of capturing this elusive quality that cities produce and make legible is not easily executed. Utility logics won't do. I can't help but think that artists are part of the answer — whether with ephemeral public performances and installations, or durable public sculpture; with site-specific/community-based art, or nomadic sculptures that circulate among localities; or indeed through architects' ability to navigate several forms of knowledge. It cannot be architecture as a hermetic dialogue between art and money. Acting on these possibilites entails architectural forms that are a kind of creative workshop open to other artistic practices and to the practices of users.

The sites for this open practice can be located in a variety of spaces, including intersections of transport and communication networks — sites where the naked eye or the engineer's imagination sees no shape, no possibility of a form, just pure infrastructure and its necessary uses. Part of the work of such an architecture and urban design lies in detecting possible architectures where now there is merely a formal silence, a non-existence. Such an architecture is thus able to navigate through more forms of expression and knowledge than an architecture of demonstration. In so doing it allows us to capture something about the elusive quality of 'urbanity' —

that compound of complexity which is missing in the theme-parking of the urban. This brings with it the possibility of making public space.

ANCHORING PUBLIC SPACE THROUGH
DIFFERENCE AND COMPLEXITY

I see this kind of architecture in several of the public projects by David Adjaye presented in this publication. The two Idea Stores, the Deptford and Tottenham centres, the Rivington Place building in Shoreditch, and the Wakefield Market Hall, are all public buildings that make public space. They do so in specific ways, through particular formal elements and materials. These buildings don't point to an elsewhere — they are not symbolising some other idealised condition, one not present in the neighbourhood. They are of the place, but they are not subsumed by it. They stand out in the urban fabric where they are inserted, and in so doing produce a point of gravity around which practices can emerge and be shaped. These buildings are not simply in public space. They *are* public space.

A critical element in these buildings is the wall. The wall here is a space of a special sort. It reminds me of what I identify as analytic borderlands in my research. These are spaces comprising what are commonly seen as discontinuous and mutually exclusive spaces. In constituting them as analytic borderlands, discontinuities are given a terrain rather than reduced to a dividing line. In this terrain, discontinuities become an integral part, a component of a space, rather than a division between two different spaces articulated around the dualities of inside/outside, private/public.[2]

If the wall does indeed function as such a border*land* rather than border*line*, then the particular materials, the visual experience, the sensory experience, all matter because they are constituting a sort of third space. In the case of Adjaye's buildings, the walls are often stunningly beautiful in their mix of precision, complexity, and sensory engagement. Each of these three features can work as sites for engaging the passer-by or the user of the building. The wall becomes a space that constitutes or activates public space, not what divides the inside from the outside.

The precision and complexity of these buildings and their walls ensure that the interactions with the surrounding space are not a form of dilution. The building, the wall and the surrounding area, each maintains its specificity. And yet, there is mutual conditioning. I would use the term imbrication to capture this particular mix of specificity and interaction, and to distinguish it from hybridity. At no point do any of these buildings and walls cease being their own particular presence, no matter the dynamism that binds them visually and that is produced through the movement of people. They can thus anchor a variety of practices that entail border crossings, including crossings perhaps not foreseen by the architect.

These public buildings are being built at a time that has seen a sharp ascendance of private authority over spaces once considered public. The increasing legibility of restrictions and displacements is politicising urban space. Most familiar, perhaps, is the impact of high-income residential and commercial gentrification over the last two decades. This has generated displacements that can feed the making of political subjectivity, but do not strengthen the sense of the civic on either side of the conflict. It is a displacement of households, non-profit uses and neighbourhood firms, that makes visible a power relationship — direct control by one side over the other as expressed in evictions or intermediated through the market. In this context, public-access space is an enormous resource, and we need more of it. But let us not confuse public-access space with public space. The latter requires making —

through the practices and the subjectivities of people.

The strength and clarity of Adjaye's public buildings may well mean that, through their practices, users of the space wind up making various types of publicness. This would take the project of making these buildings into the project of making public spaces in areas of urban fragmentation and conflict. It is not through mimicry of the surrounding area that these buildings can do so, but rather through their distinct presence in each of the areas and in their users' practices. Distinctiveness, precision and complexity can engage the subjectivity of users and passers by, drawing them even if for a moment into a less personal and private mental space. If engagements of this sort can partly dislodge the privatized subjectivity our cities are producing, then these buildings and their walls are themselves contributing diversity to the larger areas where they are sited.

MAKING GREAT PUBLIC BUILDINGS IN MODEST PUBLIC SPACES

All of Adjaye's buildings mentioned above, as well as his Museum of Contemporary Art in Denver, are sited in areas that make me think of modest public spaces. These are not monumentalised, nor are they already ritualised. This modesty itself brings to the fore the possibility of making public spaces. It allows for the details, specifics, materials of the public buildings to assume a whole new meaning as sites for engagement — whether positive or confrontational. In so doing, Adjaye's buildings open up to particular ways for making public spaces through practices, movements inside and across the buildings, and dispositions toward the specifics of building design and the materials of walls.

Several trends come together to recover practices and imaginaries about making, rather than merely accessing, public space. The first, as we have seen, is the fact itself of today's wider unsettlements of older notions of public space. These arise from the limits to making public space in monumentalised spaces, and also from the shifts towards politicising urban space and away from civic experiences in cities. Such unsettlements can then produce openings to the experience and the option of making — in this case, making publicness.

A second is the option of such making in modest public spaces, which may well be significant for recovering the possibility of strengthening urban public space. This type of making was historically critical in European cities, and took place in the interstices of Royalty and the State. It is to be distinguished from the making of grand monumentalized spaces.

A third trend is the delicate negotiation between the renewed valuing of diversity and the renewed challenges this poses to notions and experiences of the public. I see in Adjaye's buildings an interesting instance of such a negotiation. Their distinctive presence, the complexities of design and materials, the particularities of the walls, all embed diversity in the building itself. They do not create a neutral zone, emptied of distinct meanings or markers, in order to maximize some putative inclusion of all diverse groups. Rather, Adjaye's buildings move in the opposite direction. They embed a built distinctiveness that allows for a disaggregating of social/cultural/religious diversity, producing a parallel deployment of components of identities and buildings rather than wholistic and unitary presences of each. If each of the many elements in these buildings — material, colour, embedded software, patterning, textures, volumetrics — provokes engagement, together they produce a spectrum that could have the power to disaggregate — for a moment — the claustrophobias of identity, an exiting of our private mental worlds. Can built complexity be redeployed as subjective complexity? I have in mind the notion that the monolithic identities that are contributing to segment and thereby privatise the public, can be unsettled in this process and drawn into a shared temporary engagement.

DOES MULTI-SITED SPELL NETWORKED SPACES?

It is worth considering the possibility that the simultaneity of ten public projects can itself make a difference under current conditions. Such a possibility moves these architectural interventions from parallel projects to a multi-sited event. A similar shift in actual and represented meaning is increasingly at work in other domains, especially core global and digital ones. It functions as a sort of scale-up. In the case of Adjaye's ten public buildings, it signals the possibility that they constitute a whole that is more than the sum of the buildings — for instance, if each site becomes part of public imaginaries that connect to the other sites.

This raises the question of the meaning of the local in a context of globalization and digitally networked communities. Increasingly, a local place can begin to function as a microenvironment with a far larger span than its local boundaries. While such a span is usually thought of as the seamless space of digital networks, it can also be constituted through the lumpy geography of networks of localities. Can a set of parallel public buildings, with the capacities to activate public *making*, evolve into a multi-sited event that is a kind of networked public space-making? This would still be local, but with a difference — the knowledge that such making is also happening in other localities. In my own research about various types of political making I have found this mix of local action and trans-local awareness. It constitutes a distinct political subjectivity — even though we still do not know the types of politics and practices it might yield.

What I want to capture here is a very specific feature. It is the possibility of giving presence to multiple local actors, projects and imaginaries that are either somewhat 'silent' in the larger space of the city, or invisible to each other even though they may belong to the same general socio-urban group. It gets at the possibility of constructing forms of presence that are neither part of elite universalisms or 'high culture' nor, as in advertising images, part of corporate media or consumer firms.

These are some of the ways in which the notion of the local is reinvented and repositioned. Frankly, in my discipline we lack adequate vocabularies. The local is still the local, and predicated on physicality and proximity. Yet a growing number of instances of the local are not confined to a proximate physicality. It can be very local, but oriented and connected to other instances of the local across the world. So the category of the local also contains a particular version of the non-local — the global, the translocal. We need thicker vocabularies to capture this. It struck me that the simultaneity of Adjaye's ten public buildings constitutes precisely such a thicker vocabulary; one that does not lose the specificities and complexities of each particular locality even as it can push each into practical and subjective types of public-making.

Notes

1. *See Ignasi Soli Morales in his recently issued volumes of Collected Papers (Editorial Gigli, Barcelona 2004).*

2. *In the case of the political economy, this produces a terrain within which these discontinuities can be reconstituted in terms of economic operations whose properties are not merely a function of the spaces on each side (i.e., a reduction to the condition of dividing line) but also, and most centrally, of the discontinuity itself. My argument is then that such discontinuities are an integral part of the economic system.*

RES PUBLICA OR JUST A PUBLIC THING

NIKOLAUS HIRSCH

PUBLIC MATERIAL

With his public buildings, David Adjaye leaves the scale of the private house and its intimate narratives. Beyond the sheer size of these public projects, he now deals with the architectural manifestations of complex organisations and local communities. He is confronted with a public thing, a *res publica*, and with all the political connotations and ambitions related to that notion. He has to develop new typologies and to fix, as in the case of the Bernie Grant Arts Centre, the very moment in which a community manifests itself through architecture. After a condition of invisibility, a desire for change enters a phase of visibility, concretisation and solidification. It is obvious that architecture has a critical role in social and political perception. But what does 'building public things' mean? Does architecture make politics visible? Does architecture shape the public realm?

The increasing autonomy and self-reference of architectural systems has led to the construction of paradigms of extreme environmental control (such as the white cube and the black box) that define the condition of contemporary institutional building. Yet the boundaries of the system are questioned: from the exterior by new social forces, from the interior by practices which include external phenomena. The Idea Stores investigate the architectural implications of these border conflicts in order to develop new models of porosity, i.e. strategies that work with new environmental conditions of opening and closure. In this context the notion of environment operates in a double sense: on one hand, it questions the programmatic and social structure of an institution; on the other, it focuses directly on the potential of architectural material and its inherent capacities to mediate the instability of physical environments.

In Adjaye's buildings, architectural elements such as floors and walls, or the stripes of green glass that reflect the market stands on the Whitechapel Road, are interpreted as material transitions between system and environment, as boundaries that define opening and closure. Buildings like the public pavilion developed with Olafur Eliasson on the occasion of the Venice Biennale 2005, makes it clear: by using and abusing the contraction between the instability of external fluctuation and the stability of internal concentration, the material strategy generates an architecture based on different rhythms and gradual phenomena. As a tectonic detail, the material concretises different modes of perception: degrees of visual protection and exposure, rhythms of speed and slowness, noise and silence.

BEYOND SOFT AND HARD

Cities are experienced as images. Visitors bathe in images before going anywhere — scrutinising magazines, websites, videos, and so on — and then project these images onto the place, trying to adjust what they see to what they expected to see. Physical form is questioned. This transformation of the conventional understanding of the city and its buildings is usually understood as a threat to the traditional figure of the architect.

If the city is no longer a material organisation, the architect, as the very figure of the material organiser, becomes increasingly irrelevant. But not David Adjaye. Only a few architects have gone as far without betraying their physical expertise. On the contrary, his work is not about the dichotomous logics of compromise, but about an extension of architecture towards the soft material of television and radio waves and the glossy paper of fashion magazines. What many of his colleagues still see as an act of corruption of a pure (if not puritanical) discipline, is in fact an attempt to open architectural discourse to other narratives and to situate architecture in an expanded field.

Instead of an architecture that escapes into the margin, David Adjaye looks for strategies and practices that deal with modernity at large. The profession of architecture has to face the consequences of individualisation, globalisation, technology, mobility and media. Rather than dividing the world into the hard material of the thing, as in the natural sciences, and into soft material, as in the discourses of social sciences, architecture needs an approach that brings these two cultures together. Research into either the 'hard' or 'soft' qualities of an object are naturally applied in practice, but how these two cultures function together in reality and how they form a complex dynamic whole, remains ambiguous. In practice, we do not make a separation into two cultures; quite the opposite, we assume hybrid and simultaneous relations all the time. For this reason, the philosophers Michel Serres and Bruno Latour criticise the dichotomy between 'soft' and 'hard' and propose instead the notion of 'quasi-object'. The quasi-object develops a new model of knowledge that goes beyond dividing an object into two cultures. Rather than considering an object as a fact or a value, seeing it simply as a physical form or social function, this notion begins to understand the facts and values as intrinsically interdependent wholes. 'Quasi-objects are much more social', says anthropologist and philosopher Bruno Latour, 'much more fabricated, much more collective than the "hard" parts of nature, but they are in no way the arbitrary receptacles of a full-fledged society.' Following this line, a new theory of the thing would have to integrate the ideas of sharing and assembling.

TECTONICS OF SURFACE

To say that building techniques set the rhythm of architectural evolution is trivial. Less banal is the suspicion that recent developments are less focused on technology than on the organisation of a building. Building a house with a completely new construction procedure is a dream that went a long time ago. Building industries have given up the ambition to revolutionise the shell, the raw construction, and, for the last thirty years, the shell structure has fulfilled its archaic destiny. The main changes happen instead in material applications, particularly facades and surface technologies. At the centre of systems development is the problem of the skin. These new systems have nothing in common with traditional prefabrication, offering multilayered, hybrid conglomerates of material with precisely defined areas of use. In their internal structure glue plays an increasingly important role. The interface to the raw structure is controlled via sophisticated technologies that join one material to the other. Eventually, building becomes a problem of interface.

This hermetic situation hits the architect, the traditional specialist of material organisation. Distanced from the production process of a new conglomerate material that is beyond his tectonic control, he becomes a moderator of systems. The confrontation with clearly defined technical, organisational and formal options, exposes the architect to new and unusual conceptual problems. How should he understand these surrogate materials? The traditional question of material ethics, a kind of 'material honesty', might be neglected as a minor problem. More significantly, architecture has returned to a theoretical question that had occupied architects like Semper, Viollet-le-Duc and Berlage. But now, the conditions for a theory of 'clothing' have become more difficult. They have altered to such a degree that with a building like the Dirty House clothing could eventually become coating.

The topology of surfaces and the object quality of the walled body become relevant. In the attempt to decode the naked facts of space, problems of authenticity and aura move into the centre of perception. This might even create a situation in which an architect withdraws from the possibility of building a new house and works with existing, used material. Texture becomes crucial. But how dirty is the Dirty House?

Architects deal with reality, but most of the time they miss it. The city and its streets are an arsenal of metaphors for the concrete and the real. In this sense the street acts as a correction against the abstraction and neutrality of architectural systems; it seems to deliver a privileged access to reality. The aura of an existing structure is linked to a coating strategy. The external walls are coated with anti-vandal-paint; a recontextualised material, ordinarily used for lampposts and other infrastructural elements of the street. Adjaye achieves an ambiguous material status: on the one hand it is street culture, on the other its anti-graffiti gesture avoids a naïve appropriation of street culture. He describes a dilemma in which architecture manoeuvres in public space.

Adjaye/Associates, Dirty House, London, 2002.

THE RUSES OF REPRESENTATION
On the one hand architects tend to focus on the material, organising matter, afraid of connotations, narration, anxious to leave the safety of architectural language. But there is a — maybe still vague — suspicion that representation is back. The 1990s have a brought a remarkable shift in the focus of some of the most experimental practices in architecture: away from the subject of representation, meaning and language, towards those of organisation, production and technique as potential generators of form. The flow of informational tools into design practices moved an important part of the architectural debate into 'parametric design' by claiming an architecture of emergence. However, as the potentials of production increase exponentially, a gap seems to be growing between a seemingly infinite range of formal, material, and organisational possibilities and their actual performance within political, social and economic milieus. How can the ever-expanding world of productions be re-territorialised? How should these products relate to power structures, social strata and cultural iconography? What should be the concerns of architectures, cities and objects when they are brought to the public realm? The old question of whether buildings should be pure material emergences of production, or whether they should also contain references to external value systems, be structured by languages and conventions, or relate to iconographies beyond their mere organisational nature has reappeared with renewed force.

Much architecture of the 1990s appears now lifeless, stuck in the dead end of tautology, looking like early predecessors of the parametric driven strategies that have filled architecture magazines of late. Adjaye's material, as it appears in the atmospheres of the Nobel Peace Center, the Idea Stores and the first models of the Museum of Contemporary Art in Denver, is more difficult to grasp. It has to do with opportunism, superficiality, ruse, narration and appropriation — and turns these clichés into a quality. The material strategy gives hints, but does not translate. The process of design is no exculpatory science (or pseudo-science), but an almost Nietzschean *gaya scienza*.

1

NORWAY
□ Oslo

Nobel Peace Center
City Hall Square, Oslo, Norway

Alfred Nobel, 1833–1896

Following the directions in Alfred Nobel's will, the Peace Prize is awarded annually by a committee of five people appointed by the Norwegian government. The first prize was awarded in 1901 and the presentation ceremony takes place in Oslo's City Hall. The purpose of the Nobel Peace Center is to present the history of the Peace Prize and to explain the work of its laureates. According to Grete Jarmund, who was responsible for the planning stage of this project, 'We recognized early on that this would not be a traditional museum with artefacts. Our method will be to bring small and large conflicts into the public eye.' The global diversity of the Peace Prize, combined with a desire to create a centre that is dynamic and aesthetically cohesive, also underpinned the decision.

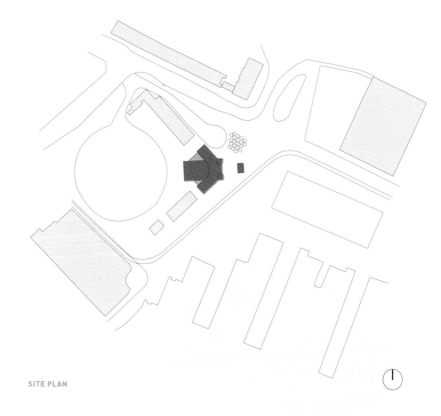

SITE PLAN

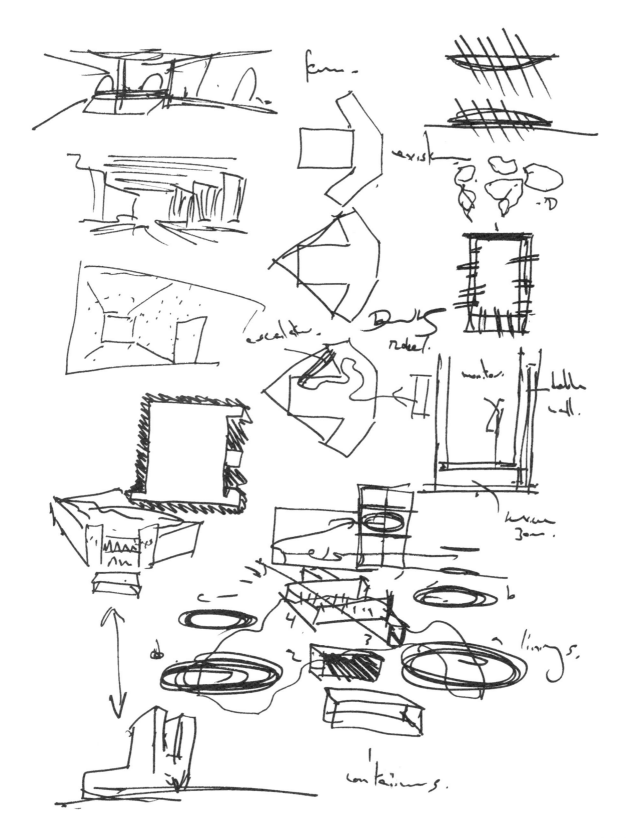

Village house, Dogon
Unique spaces contained within a powerful volume.

The Center is located in the old Vestbanen station which has similar qualities to a Dogon house: a strong external form encloses a number of highly differentiated spaces within a masonry structure. Where the original spaces are visible, they have been transformed by radical decoration. In other places the interiors have been reoccupied by a series of installations whose materiality and orientation contrast with the enclosing fabric. Whichever approach has been used, the overall intention remains the same: to create a powerful sequence of experiences which illustrate the work of the Peace Prize programme.

Area Schedule

400m² Exhibition Space
140m² Nobel Field
130m² Entrance/Register
125m² Reception/Bookshop
120m² Gallery Space
115m² Café
115m² Nobel Chamber
95m² Passage of Honour
70m² Education/Conference Rooms
60m² Living Area
55m² Kitchen
40m² Cinema

Total Area 1465m²

Materials

Sandblasted aluminium Canopy   GRP Register   Red resin Reception   Grey felt Auditorium   Polished brass cladding Passage of Honour   Cedar wood timber cladding Temporary Gallery   Blue rubber flooring Nobel Field   Coloured glass interlayer Nobel Field

Site Concept

Existing building

The old Vestbanen railway station has symmetrical wings, at right angles to each other, and is entered on the diagonal axis.

Canopy

Standing in front of the main entrance, the canopy signals that there has been a change in use of the original building.

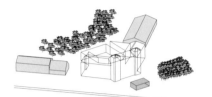

Register

Situated just inside the entrance, the register introduces the main themes of the centre, peace and conflict.

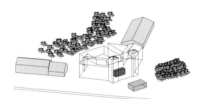

Reception and Café de la Paix

To the right side of the entrance, the reception area leads to the first in a series of distinctive installations. On the left of the entrance, a café is located at the end of this sequence.

Passage of Honour

This space celebrates the work of the current Nobel peace laureate. It is positioned along one side of the temporary exhibition space and connects the reception area to an escalator which leads to the first floor.

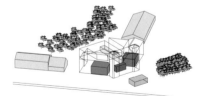

Nobel Field

This installation reveals the diversity of the Nobel peace laureates and how their work has made a vital contribution in a wide range of situations.

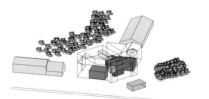

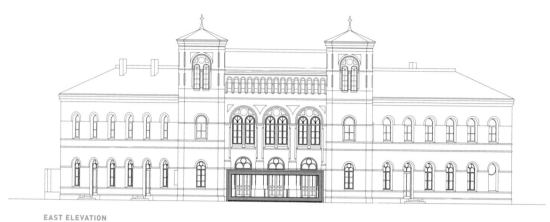

EAST ELEVATION

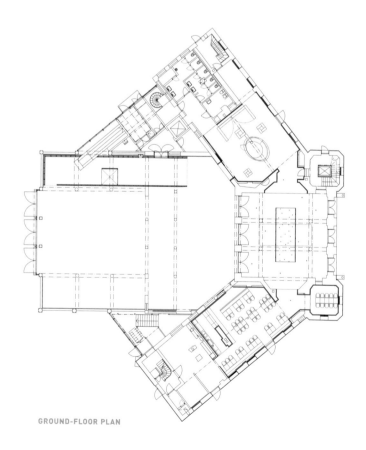

GROUND-FLOOR PLAN

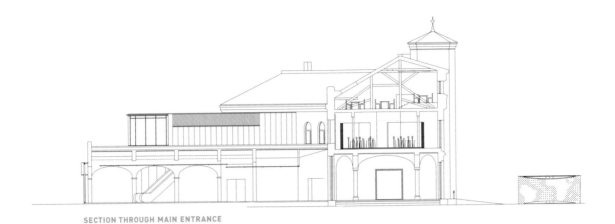

SECTION THROUGH MAIN ENTRANCE

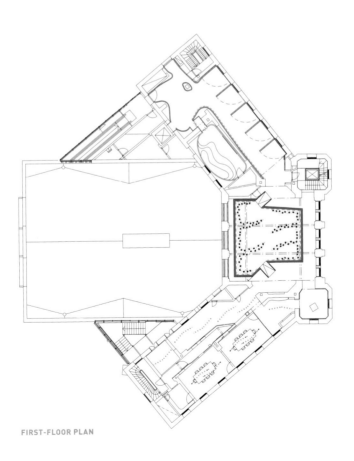

FIRST-FLOOR PLAN

Assembly of volumes

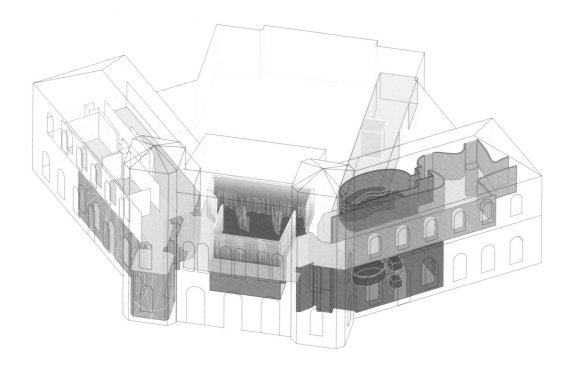

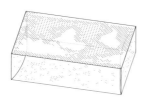

- ● Register Tunnel
- ● Reception
- ● Cinema and Exhibition
- ● Passage of Honour
- ● Nobel Field
- ● Cafe

Canopy

Each of the installations functions as a threshold between its immediate neighbours. The canopy introduces this theme before entering the building. It brings together two architectural elements which normally lead separate lives: the gateway or portal and the type of arching footway which is associated with bridges. Constructed of unpolished aluminium, the pattern of holes represents the main land masses of the world; this is most clearly visible when seen from inside the main building. There are lights within the void of the footway.

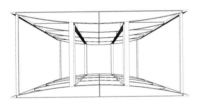

SECTION

STRUCTURE

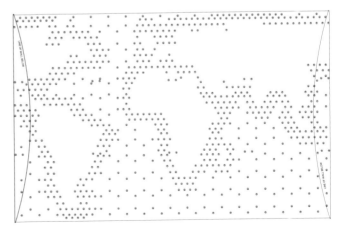

ROOF PLAN

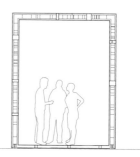

CROSS SECTION

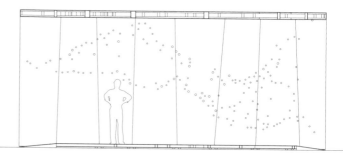

LONG SECTION

Register

The position of the register interacts with the movement of visitors into the building and directs them to the spaces on each side of the entrance. Constructed in grp, it forms an 8m long tunnel. Holes on the inner face represent the positions of major cities around the world and each one emits a green or red light, according to whether they are in a state of peace or conflict. The holes also emit the sound of voices speaking in the language of that city. Close to, the voices can be heard separately; collectively, they produce a soft ambient sound.

Reception

To acknowledge the role of conflict in their programme, the reception area is coloured red, with a resin finish to all surfaces, furniture and storage. The use of colour unites the new elements with the fabric of the original building. The reception desk consists of a tapered oval volume and, as if to greet each visitor, it leans towards the entrance. At times when the café is open but the rest of the building is closed, the bookshelves fold shut and the small display units can be moved to a secure location.

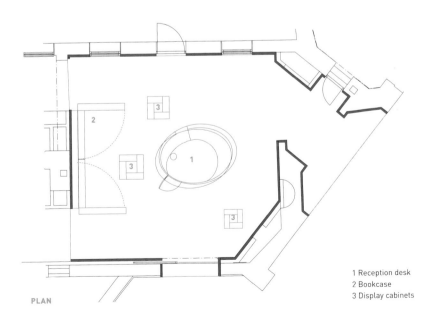

PLAN

1 Reception desk
2 Bookcase
3 Display cabinets

Exhibition Space and Cinema

There are two spaces for temporary exhibitions. The larger one is designed as a black box and is located on axis with the main entrance. The smaller one, for more informal exhibitions, is on the first floor. The floor, walls and ceiling are lined in Cedar wood and the windows can be closed off by full-height pivoting panels. When the windows are not covered, the panels can be positioned at right angles to the wall creating five bays. There is a small cinema next to this space.

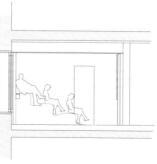

SECTION THROUGH CINEMA

Above
Exhibition space.
Temporary gallery.

Left
Cinema space.

Nobel Prize medal

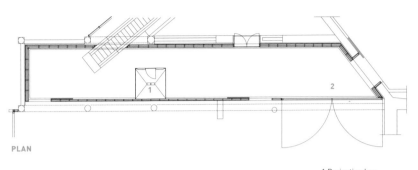

PLAN

1 Projection box
2 Rotatable walls

Passage of Honour

From reception, the visitor has the choice of moving into the temporary exhibition hall or the Passage of Honour, which celebrates the work of the most recent Nobel peace laureate. The larger horizontal tube which forms this space is divided into two parts by a small vertical tube whose sides include two screens for the back projection of a video presentation of the laureate's work. The floor, walls and ceiling of the tunnel are clad with sheets of brass and the video image is reflected several times over, an effect which represents the gathering momentum of the laureate's work in the outside world. There are two lighting slots, at floor and ceiling level, as well as the light from the projection itself.

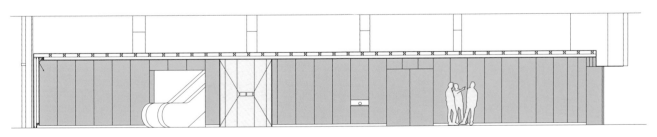

LONG SECTION

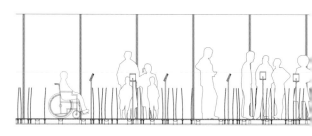

SECTION OF MONITOR AND LED LIGHT

PART SECTION

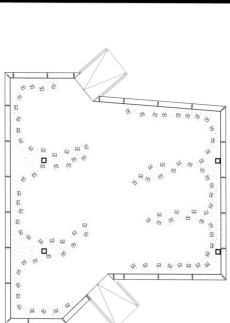

PLAN

Nobel Field

This space provides the concluding presentation on the Peace Prize programme. It is more static than the other installations and is situated directly above the main entrance. The title refers to the manner in which each of the Peace Prize laureates is represented by a monitor standing on a clear acrylic support. At rest, the monitor displays a portrait of that person but, when approached by a visitor, it switches into a video presentation of his or her work. The dark blue colour of the floor, walls and ceiling focuses attention on the monitors and, together with a sound installation composed by Peter Adjaye, contributes to a calm and reflective atmosphere.

Café de la Paix

In contrast to the reception area, the café is painted in different shades of green. The mural *Earth Minor Major in Yellow and Green*, by the artist Chris Ofili, is a spatial version of the maps on which airlines represent their flights by drawing a line between different destinations. As in the reception space, decoration, rather than installation, is the means of adapting the existing building to its new role.

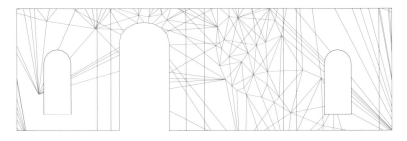

DINING ROOM, INTERNAL ELEVATION AND REFLECTED CEILING PLAN

VIDSYN · BROADMINDEDNESS

Above
Looking from Register
towards Reception.

Right
Looking from Reception
to the Passage of Honour.

Previous page
Canopy, looking towards
entrance.

TOGHALLEN
THE MAIN HALL

Above
The Entrance Hall
and Register.

Right
Looking towards the
Café de la Paix from
the entrance.

Left and above
Nobel Field.

Following page
The canopy looking
towards City Hall.

2

HACKNEY

□ **Shoreditch**

L O N D O N

Rivington Place
1 Rivington Street, Shoreditch

Rivington Place, 2003–2007

Stuart Hall

This building has been designed to meet the requirements of two organisations with parallel agendas. Autograph ABP was established in 1988 and is a photographic arts agency with an international audience. Its primary role is to develop, exhibit and publish the work of photographers and artists from culturally diverse backgrounds and to advocate their inclusion in all areas of exhibition, publishing, education and commerce in the visual arts. The Institute for International Visual Arts was founded in 1994 to promote the work of artists, academics and curators from a plurality of cultural backgrounds, to introduce innovative art practice to new audiences, and to extend the intellectual, social and geographic boundaries of debate on contemporary visual art. The distinguished cultural theorist Stuart Hall has played a formative role in relation to both Autograph and inIVA .

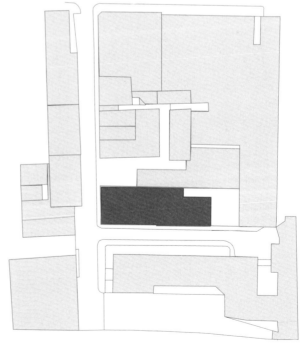

SITE PLAN

Sowei mask, Sierra Leone
A repeated unit changes size to match the geometry of the surface.

The site is located in Shoreditch where the historic fabric, including many warehouses, has been re-colonised by a variety of cultural organisations and small businesses. The building which previously occupied the site has been demolished but the volume of the new building has similar proportions to some of the warehouses in the area. The materiality and colouring are intended to update the architectural language of the older buildings whilst being responsive to the requirements and general considerations presented by the brief.

Area Schedule

Offices 600m²	
Circulation 320m²	
Project Space 300m²	
Library 90m²	
Bar/Café 50m²	
Workshop/Storage 45m²	
Multimedia 45m²	

Total Area 1445m²

Materials

Polished concrete   Pre-cast concrete   Concrete   High gloss steel   Clear glass

Site concept

Location

The site is located in an area of narrow streets and is surrounded by buildings.

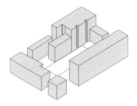

Volume

In order to provide the accommodation required, it is necessary to develop most of the site to the height of the neighbouring buildings.

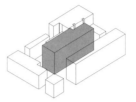

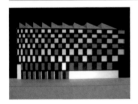

Atrium

The building is entered through a three-storey high atrium which is positioned half way down its long side.

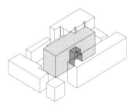

Cuts

At either end, the main volume is cut back at ground level in order to engage with the external conditions.

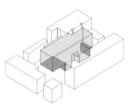

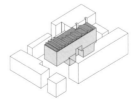

Roof

The roof is constructed of metal and terminates the vertical composition.

Facade

The external conditions on the outward facing edges of the site are different in each case but a single facade system has been applied to both.

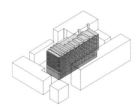

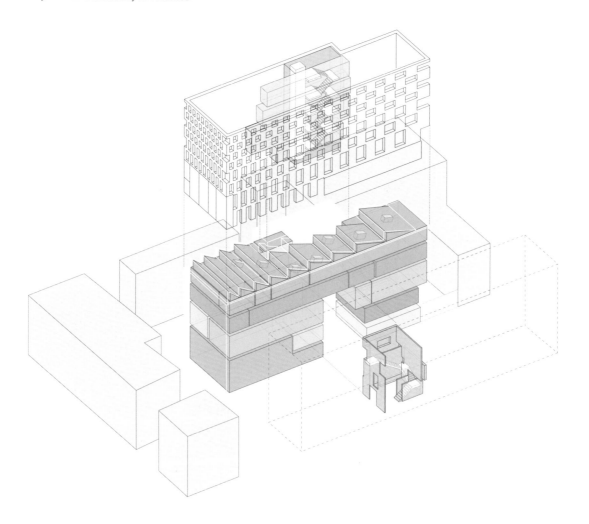

The occupation of the section becomes more dense moving from ground level to the top storey. The public spaces are accessed from the atrium, with offices on the floors above. The external facade is punctuated by rectangular openings positioned within an expanding grid. The openings on the front elevation are the same width, but a different height, at each level. On the side elevation, both dimensions are changeable.

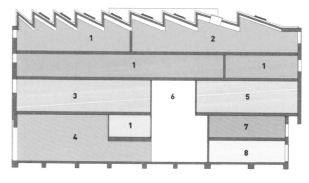

LONG SECTION

1 Office space
2 Studio space
3 Library
4 Project space 1
5 Project space 2
6 Atrium
7 Interactive space
8 Cafe

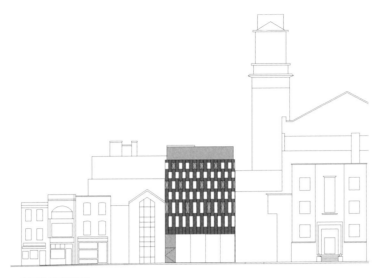

SOUTH ELEVATION

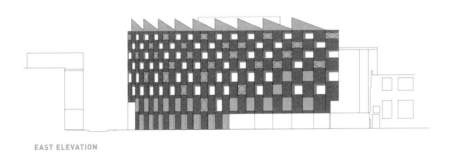

EAST ELEVATION

SOUTH AND EAST FACADES

GROUND-FLOOR PLAN

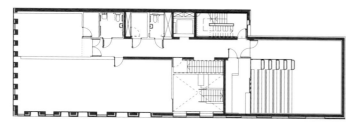

SECOND-FLOOR PLAN

The effect of the facade system on the internal spaces varies in different parts of the building. It is not unusual for spaces to have windows at two different levels, the lower ones giving views into the street and the upper ones giving views of the sky. In the larger spaces, the windows produce an ambiguous sense of scale as their position and size contradict the effects of perspective. The section and the plan of the Project Space 1 space increase in scale, moving from the entrance towards the street.

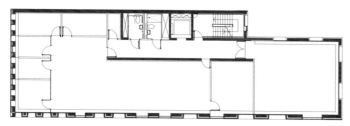

THIRD-FLOOR PLAN

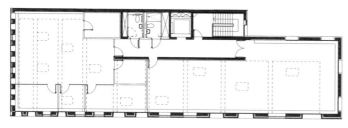

FOURTH-FLOOR PLAN

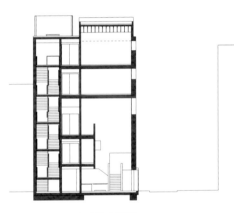

ATRIUM LOOKING DOWN

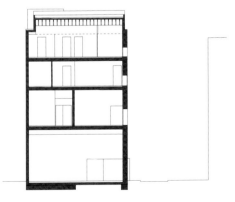

SECTION THROUGH PROJECT SPACE 1

The short side of the site faces a through street and, at ground level, Project Space 1 is located here for maximum exposure. The long side of the site is on a short *cul de sac*, the amount of vehicular traffic is limited, and the space beyond the entrance is occupied by a cafe. In both of these locations, the external walls are fully glazed. Although the roof mimics the north-light section found on industrial buildings, the rooflights are not positioned on the vertical planes.

PROJECT SPACE 1

TOP FLOOR LOOKING NORTH

To achieve column-free spaces, the southern section of the building has a clear span of 11.4m supported on concrete walls. The solid sections of wall have an external cladding of dark-coloured precast concrete panels with a shallow, box-like section. Their open sides, towards the interior, are used to house the insulation which is necessary to achieve the required thermal performance. The precast units are connected at their corners and the openings have deep reveals. The windows are positioned on the inside face and there are insulated steel panels, with a reflective finish, on the outside face. On the short facade, the pattern of the openings exaggerates the vertical perspective, making the building seem higher. On the long facade, the pattern of the openings contradicts the horizontal perspective, making the building appear shorter than it is.

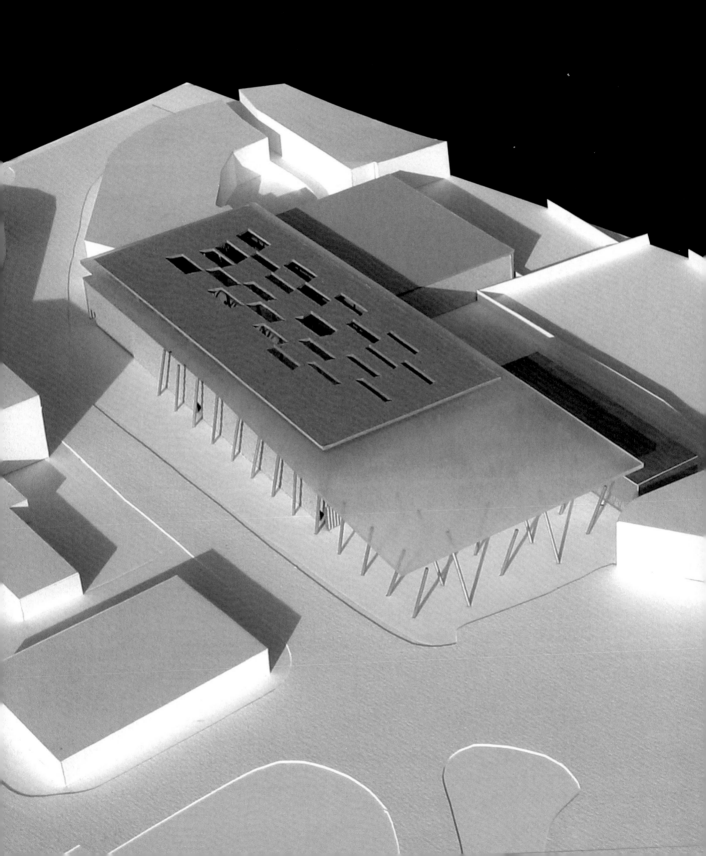

3

GREAT BRITAIN

□ **Wakefield**

Wakefield Market Hall
Marshway, Wakefield, West Yorkshire

Wakefield Market, 2005–2007

This project is close to the centre of town: there is a bus station to the north, an art gallery to the east, and the main square and an imposing church are a short distance away to the south. The public sections of the market, the dry goods hall and a smaller food hall, frame two sides of a covered square. From the bus station, this space acts as a portico to the town centre. On the opposite corner, a cleared site awaits the next phase of the Marsh Way development, of which the market is phase one.

SITE PLAN

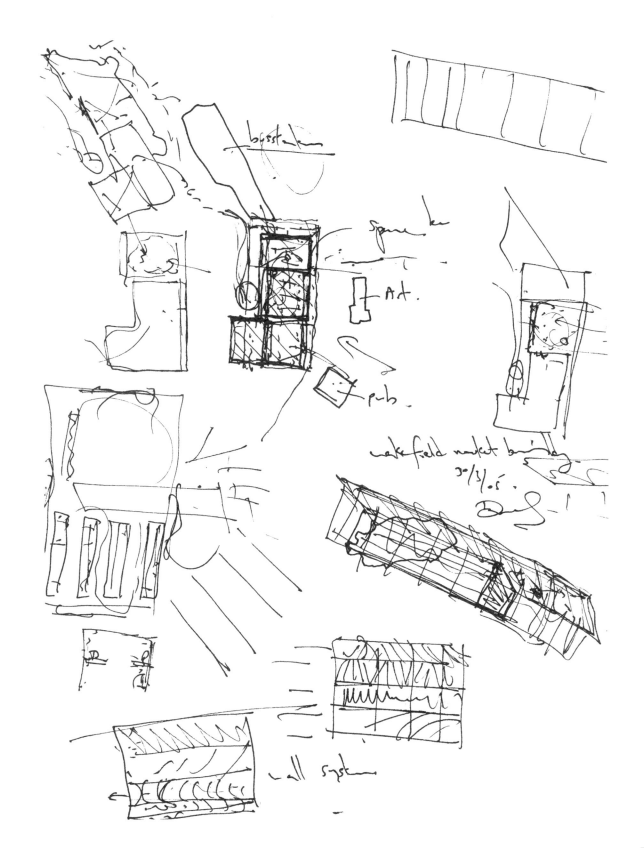

bus station

space be

Art.

pub.

wakefield market bn'
30/3/05.

wall system

Sunshade, Mali
Irregular tree trunks supporting a flat roof.

The complete market consists of three halls which are related to one another by a large flat roof supported on a steel frame. With this plane as the dominant reference, the relative positions of the halls define two open spaces: a public square and a service yard. Each of the halls has different proportions and a distinctive materiality. The experience of moving between a number of fully and partially enclosed spaces is one of continuous change and contrast.

Area Schedule

Market Hall 1790m² (Retail Units 290m², Retail Stalls 440m², Open Plan Sales Area 930m², Cafe Point 20m², Administration 20m², Ancillary 90m²)	
Market Square 890m²	
Storage Building 830m²	
Food Hall 450m² (Retail Stalls 190m², Open Plan Sales Area 200m², Ancillary 60m²)	
Total Area 3960m²	

Materials

Laminated veneer lumber   Heat treated timber   Concrete paving   Splitface block   Powdercoated Steel   Clear polycarbonate   Translucent polycarbonate

Site concept

Site plan

The site occupies a transitional zone between the town centre and the surrounding area. It is well served by local roads whilst providing an extensive pedestrian environment.

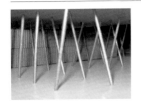

Columns

Parallel rows of columns, leaning like trees in a wood, define a volume of space with civic proportions .

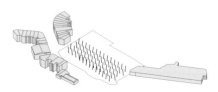

Market Hall

In relation to the main hall, the external columns form a peristyle to the north and an arcade to the east, providing a covered link between the bus station and the town centre.

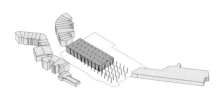

Food Hall and Ancillary building

These two buildings enclose opposite sides of a generous service yard and the food hall makes a back wall to the new public space.

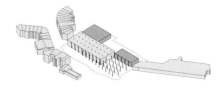

Roof structure

The heads of the square steel columns are linked by steel beams with the same dimensions. The secondary structure consists of structural veneer lumber beams.

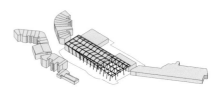

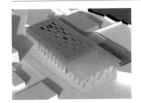

Canopy

The canopy over the public space is covered with translucent polycarbonate sheets and the dry goods hall has a solid roof with rooflights.

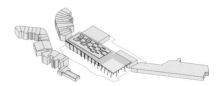

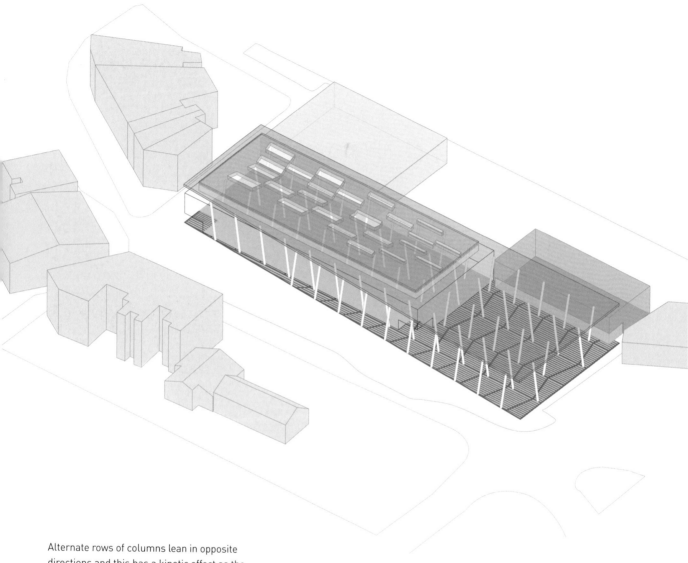

Alternate rows of columns lean in opposite
directions and this has a kinetic effect as the
angles appear to vary when seen from different
positions. This theme is continued in the public
square where the the organisation of the roof
structure is reflected in the pattern of the floor
below in two shades of grey tiles. When the sun
shines through the roof, the shadows repeat
this pattern in a different position. In the main
hall each stall has its own lighting. The level of
natural lighting is graduated from north to
south as the size of the rooflights increases.

The walling system for the dry goods hall consists of large panels of laminated timber. The laminations are vertical but a series of horizontal grooves, more closely spaced at mid-height, have been routed out of the external face. At the back of the main hall, the dry store is constructed of concrete blocks with deeply raked joints. The walls of the food hall are constructed from concrete paving slabs which have been broken in half. They are laid in horizontal courses, like dry-stone walling, with the broken edges to the outside and the square edges to the inside.

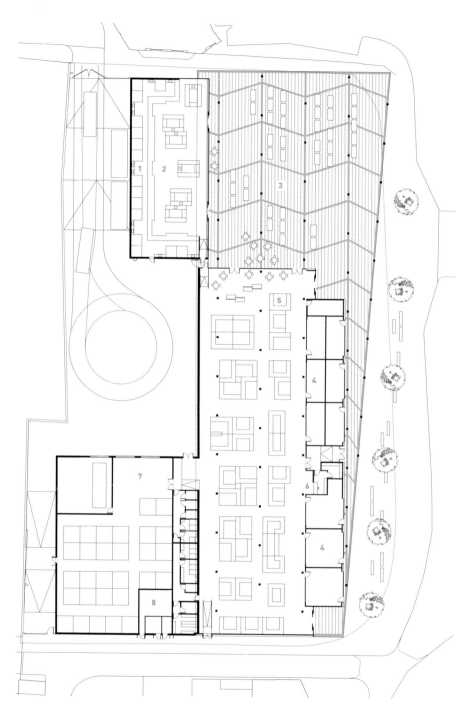

1 Retail stalls
2 Open plan sales area
3 Market square
4 Retail units
5 Cafe point
6 Administration
7 Dry Goods Store
8 Plant

GROUND-FLOOR PLAN

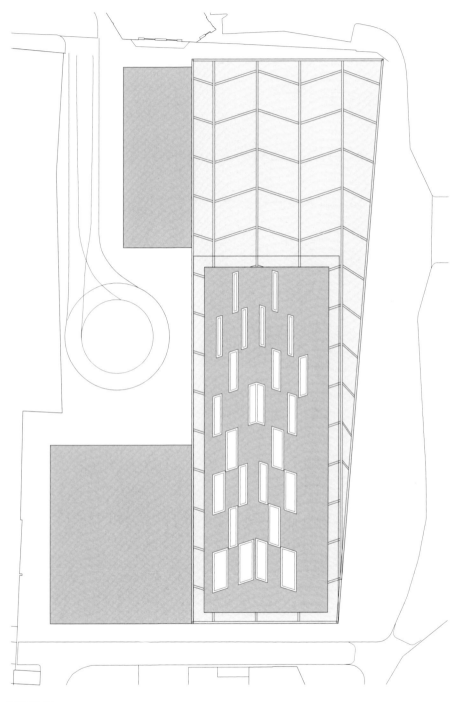

ROOF PLAN

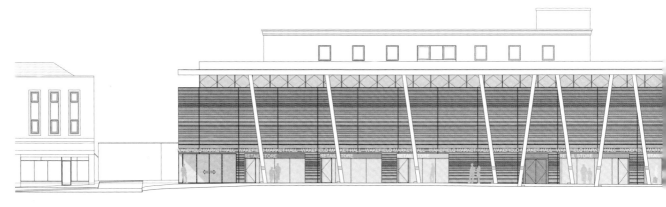

EAST ELEVATION

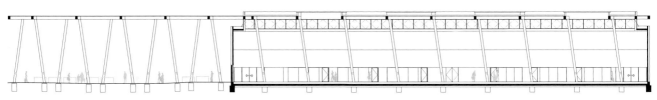

SECTION THROUGH MAIN HALL

SECTION THROUGH MEAT AND FISH HALL

Despite different uses, the horizontal bands of each facade continue the scale
and visual organisation of the neighbouring buildings. Together with the lines
of the main roof, they strengthen the connection between the new market and
its surroundings, and suggest a future link with the second phase of the Marsh
Way development.

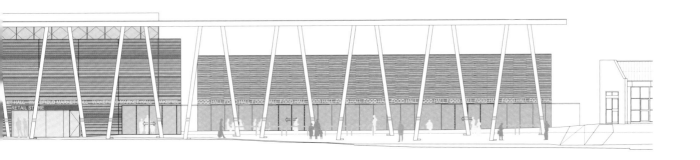

MATERIALS AND MATERIALITY

PETER ALLISON

Adjaye/Associates, LxWxH Pavilion, Rivington Place, London, 2004.

In 2004 Adjaye/Associates completed *LxWxH*, a temporary pavilion whose organisation and materiality exemplify their practice. In this project, an elevated rectangular tube occupied the long axis of the site for the Rivington Place building in Shoreditch. The structure of the tube consisted of closely-spaced frames of laminated timber. They supported a timber floor, as well as walls and ceiling panels of plywood or grp(glass-reinforced plastic); the width of the grp panels was the same as the distance between two vertical frames, while the solid panels were the same width or a multiple of it. On the outside, the panels formed a continuous surface and the solid sections were painted black, in contrast to the stripes of translucent grp. On the inside, the frames were seen as a series of fins, the solid sections were painted white except for the sections of the floor which corresponded with the positions of the grp panels: they were painted grey. The pavilion could be entered through openings in opposite side walls at each end of the tube. They were approached by ramps and, as the south end was higher than the north end, it required a longer ramp. Each end was clad with a single sheet of glass and focussed attention on the external conditions at that end of the site.

The experience of moving through the tube was complicated by its gentle incline, which distorted the internal perspective, as well as by the greater frequency of translucent panels towards the two ends, which appeared to reduce the distances involved in these sections. In using the entrance and exit ramps and making a single journey through the pavilion, it was necessary to walk twice the length of the site. Both *LxWxH* and another pavilion designed by Adjaye/Associates, *Asymmetric Chamber*, demonstrate an intense interest in tube-like spaces whose edges are supported by vertical fins.[1] In *LxWxH* the spatial experience is modified by changes in the pattern of solid and translucent panels, an arrangement that also plays a key role in the two Idea Stores which Adjaye/Associates have now completed.

At Chrisp Street, a spine wall on the main floor has the effect of reducing the width of a space which was already the length of the site. Both internally and externally, the length is measured out in units of 1700mm: the combined width of the 600mm and 1100mm glass panels which form the east facade. On the inside, the positions of the junctions between the glass panels are marked by fins of laminated timber which give the wall the stiffness to resist wind loading and support bookshelves, worktops and seats. As in the pavilions, using the library involves a series of journeys parallel to this wall. The entrance can only be approached by walking along the east facade and, from this position, the glass is difficult to see through. It reflects the immediate context and the sky, and the effect of the coloured glass is muted. Inside the main library space, there are two continuous routes. The first is located next to the wall that divides the main space from the teaching spaces: from this position, the east facade presents a changeful sequence of external views as the solid and coloured panels form a series of flexible frames. The second route is immediately next to the facade and is one of sharp contrasts, depending on whether it offers an external view or access to library facilities mounted on the wall.

The structure of the Chrisp Street Idea Store consists of a grid of steel columns that supports the roof. The facade system hangs from the edge of this structure. In a simple version, the enclosure provided by these elements would consist of a long rectangular box. In its built form, the box has been subjected to the specificity of the site, as described in the Site Concept drawings for this project (p. 163). One end of the volume has been tapered in plan and section and, to compensate for these losses, the height of the central section of the library space has been increased. In this way, the systems that form the basic enclosure at Chrisp Street have been customised in order to address the conditions on each side of the site.

A similar process informs the design of the external wall. The glass panels come in widths that take account of the processes of production and assembly of the wall itself and, at the same time, their dimensions provide appropriate widths for supporting elements of the library. The glass panels, which are sometimes made opaque by areas of insulation, have similar qualities to the type of screen walls found in traditional Japanese architecture. Their repetition suggests horizontal movement whilst their vertical proportions suggest repose. As the interior of Chrisp Street Idea Store is intended to encourage people to move between facilities and to provide opportunities for private study, the combination of these qualities is particularly appropriate.

In the Whitechapel Idea Store, tubular spaces appear in many guises and provide all of the public spaces on each floor of the adult library. To the south, they look onto the suspended atrium; to the north, they look onto the supermarket car park; to the east, they are wider and have views of the neighbouring building; to the west, they form book-lined galleries of varying widths. The suspended atrium takes the form of a tapered tube that draws people to the second floor entrance where the automatic door reveals a narrow linear space, three-storeys high and linking the floors of the main library. In this project, a concrete frame has been modified by removing a substantial volume along the northern edge of the site, and forming a cantilever to the east, in concrete, and a cantilever to the south, in steel. In this way, the specificity of the site has been addressed by the customization of the structure.

Tube-like spaces with one solid and one open edge, and with vertical supports at rhythmic intervals, can be found in various types of historic architecture, most commonly in the arcaded spaces found on the edges of buildings in many cultures. The pattern of linear spaces located on either side of a central core and leading into a deeper enclosure was a twentieth century development. A notable example is the design of Crown Hall, designed for the Architecture Department at the Illinois Institute of Technology, Chicago, by the German architect Mies van der Rohe and completed in 1956. In this building, the external walls hang from the roof and are extensively glazed. The components which provide stiffness to these walls are steel I-sections located on the outside face of

MATERIALS BY TYPE, TEXTURE AND COLOUR

Glass	Wood	Composite wood	Stone	Plastic	Metal	Pressed metal
Laminated green glass	Purpleheart wood	Wood fibre board	Polished concrete	GRP	Sandblasted aluminium	Metal ridgidal
Laminated blue glass	Spruce Plywood	Perforated parklex timber cladding	Pre-cast concrete	Red resin	Polished brass cladding	Perforated steel
Laminated clear glass	Cedar	Wood wool	Concrete	Blue rubber flooring	High gloss steel	Expanded metal mesh
Coloured glass interlayer	Pressure treated timber	Laminated veneer lumber	Concrete paving	Clear/translucent polycarbonate	Powder coated steel	
Grey glass	Heat treated timber	Orientated strand board	Splitface block	Monopan	Brass	
Glass panels	Paralex timber cladding		Grey slate	Green rubber flooring	Weathered brass	
	Grey stained redwood		Sienna slate	Red rubber flooring	Bronze	
			Grey/green slate	Bituminous fibre board	Weathered bronze	
				Mastic asphalt	Anodised aluminium	

the building. Following recent practice, Adjaye /Associates have placed the stiffening elements on the inside face of the Idea Store walls and use them to support library facilities. In referring to his buildings as forms of imbrication, this is the type of layering that Adjaye has in mind.

Aluminium is one of the materials used for the structure of curtain wall systems and in the Idea Store buildings there is a small aluminium section that provides a two-way connection between the panels of the curtain wall and the timber fins. The addition of timber to the normal combination of materials is one of the most significant details in both buildings. Without the timber fins, the materiality and colouring of the curtain wall would be visually cool on both faces. With the timber fins, the outside face of the wall remains cool while the inside face, taking into account the effect of the coloured glass, is transformed into an assembly of materials that is visually warm. This detail, in other words, precipitates the difference between the exterior and the interior of these projects. From the outside, they have a largely abstract presence that, despite their proportions and colouring, is entirely deferential to their surroundings. The interiors, in contrast, are warm and colourful, presenting a range of possibilities whilst maintaining a welcoming and informal atmosphere.[2]

The polarisation of conditions can be seen throughout Adjaye's *oeuvre* and appears to conform to a principle of complementary opposites. At Chrisp Street, the contrast between the scale and monumentality of the entrance space and the intimate character of the northern end of the library space establishes a spatial tension that conditions the patterns of occupation occurring between these poles. At the Whitechapel Idea Store, the organisation of the section is based on the contrast between conditions at street and roof levels: using the building inevitably involves a journey from one condition to the other.

The same principle plays a significant role in the selection of materials for each project. The installations for the Nobel Peace Center are predominantly warm in colour, if not texture, but they start on a cool note – with the aluminium canopy and grp register – and end with the luxurious blue atmosphere of the Nobel Field. At the Bernie Grant Arts Centre, the choice of Purpleheart timber for the cladding of the auditorium building, and the lining of the entrance space, is supported by the use of cool systems, ceramic tiles and aluminium panels on the other buildings. In The Wakefield Market Hall, the continuity of the structural frame, in steel and timber, is complemented by the spatial and material specificity of the three halls. In the projects that will present contemporary art, the Rivington Place building and the Museum of Contemporary Art in Denver, a limited number of monochromatic materials contribute to the creation of environments that will be hospitable to a wide range of art works. In the Art Pavilion in Venice, the use of a warm palette of materials, timber, timber products and bituminous sheet, is a precise complement to the predominant colouring of the site, inflected by the Venetian sky and the laguna. In each case, a range of materials has been carefully brought together in response to programme and context. As David Adjaye has commented, 'Once you understand the proposal and what is being said, each material plays its correct part within the scenography of the whole'.

Notes

1. *Asymmetric Chamber, CUBE Manchester, 2003, CUBE Liverpool, 2003–04, and Bohen Foundation, New York, 2004–05. The walls of Asymmetric Chamber were supported by laminated timber fins at non-standard centres.*

2. *The movement from warm to cool is sometimes managed in steps. In the library spaces at the Whitechapel Idea Store, the red floor is the most warm, followed in stages by the external wall, the concrete ceiling and the long walls of the central core, which are the most cool.*

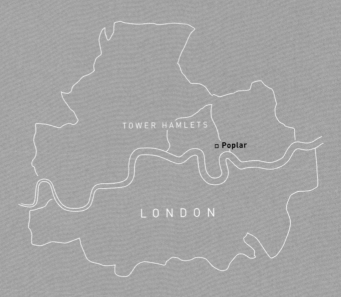

TOWER HAMLETS

□ **Poplar**

L O N D O N

4

Fairfield Road Housing
101–109 Fairfield Road, London

The client for this project is Presentation, a
social investment agency, with a requirement for
46 affordable homes. Of these, 31 will be rented
and 15 will be in shared ownership, where the
occupants own a proportion of their apartment
and pay rent on the remainder. The latter option
gives individuals and young families an opportunity
to move towards full ownership when this would
not be possible on the open market. Thirty units
have two bedrooms and twelve units, intended for
larger families, have three or four bedrooms. The
larger units are situated in a two-storey podium
and the remainder are accommodated within two
closely-spaced towers.

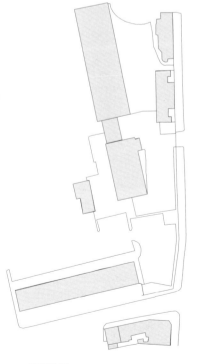
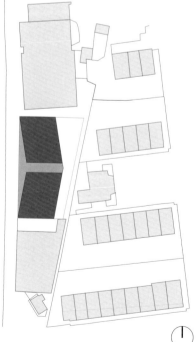

SITE PLAN

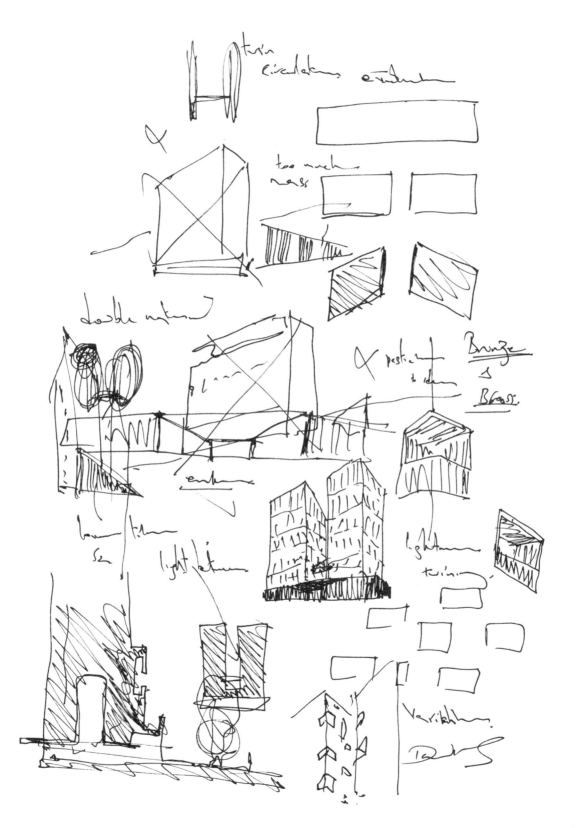

Gold weight, Ghana
Parallel edges create a tension between two bodies.

Area Schedule

Living Area Rented 2370m²	
Living Area Shared Ownership 1045m²	
Communal Area 535m²	
Garden Terrace 270m²	
Balcony 55m²	
Total Area 4275m²	

Immediately to the west of the site is the Bow Quarter, a conservation area where the majority of buildings are constructed in a red London stock brick. In other directions, many buildings make use of a yellow brick. The materials selected for the external cladding refer to the existing situation, as well as taking their place within a contemporary form of construction. With weathering, the bronze cladding on the north tower will match the brickwork of the conservation area and the brass cladding on the southern tower will correspond with the yellow brickwork of the other buildings.

Materials

Brass　　Weathered brass　　Bronze　　Weathered bronze　　Parklex timber cladding　　Perforated parklex timber cladding　　Cedar wood

Site Concept

Volume

The site is located in a mixed-height residential area. The older buildings are relatively low and more recent developments are higher.

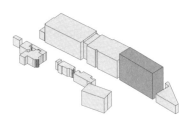

Division

In order to reduce the impact of the developable volume on the surrounding area, it is divided into two equal parts.

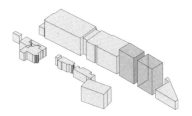

Angle

In order to soften the impact of the main facades on the surrounding area, the two blocks are set at an angle to one another. This creates a shallow forecourt and improves the views in the vicinity of the site.

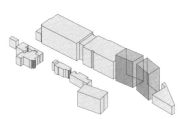

Podium

The height of the older buildings on Fairfield Road is acknowledged by the proportions of the podium, giving a sense of continuity between buildings constructed at different times.

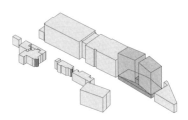

Cladding

The cladding materials respond to the conditions around the site and the use of bronze and brass for the towers reduces their volumes to a series of reflective planes.

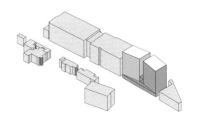

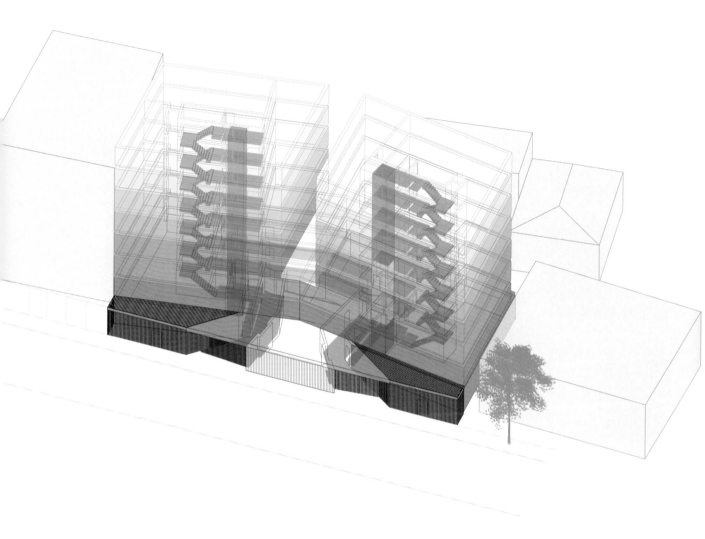

The larger apartments in the lower floors are designed to be fully accessible for wheelchair users and each of them has its own external space at ground level or on the deck at first floor level. There is no difference between the rented units and those in shared ownership, apart from their position: the northern tower is devoted exclusively to the shared ownership units. It was a client requirement that there should be a separate entrance to these units and this is the reason that the building has two entrances.

CROSS SECTION LOOKING SOUTH

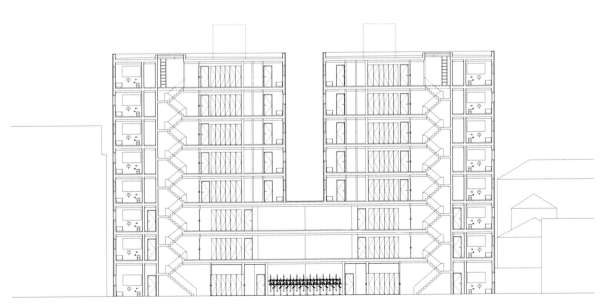

LONG SECTION

GROUND-FLOOR PLAN

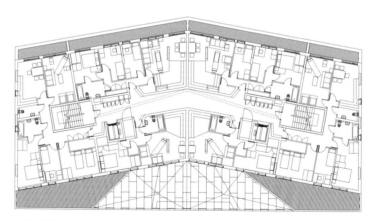

FIRST-FLOOR PLAN

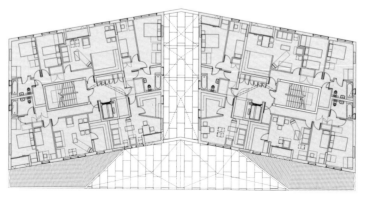

THIRD-FLOOR PLAN

1 Living Room
2 Kitchen / Dining
3 WC
4 En-suite Bathroom
5 Master Bedroom
6 Hall
7 Bedroom 1
8 Bedroom 2
9 Bedroom 3
10 Storage
11 Front Garden
12 Rear Garden
13 Open Kitchen
14 Living / Dining
15 Terrace
16 Winter Garden
17 Bathroom
18 Kitchen

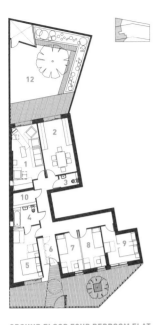

GROUND FLOOR FOUR BEDROOM FLAT

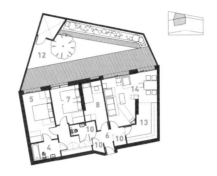

GROUND FLOOR THREE BEDROOM FLAT

FIRST FLOOR THREE BEDROOM FLAT

FIRST FLOOR THREE BEDROOM FLAT

FIRST FLOOR ONE BEDROOM FLAT

THIRD FLOOR TWO BEDROOM FLAT

THIRD FLOOR TWO BEDROOM FLAT

THIRD FLOOR TWO BEDROOM FLAT

WEST ELEVATION

EAST ELEVATION

CROSS SECTION ON CENTRAL AXIS

The gap between the two towers plays a significant role in improving the natural light on both sides of the project. In summer, the rising sun is able to shine through the open slot into Primrose Close, to the west of the site. In the middle of the day, the sun shines through the project from the other direction, into Fairfield Road. The ground and first floors are clad in Parklex, a timber weather-board which provides a warm finish, where the exterior is experienced at close quarters, and unifies the podium without increasing the perception of mass. The unit plans repeat on alternate floors, reproducing the vertical rhythm of a two-storey building.

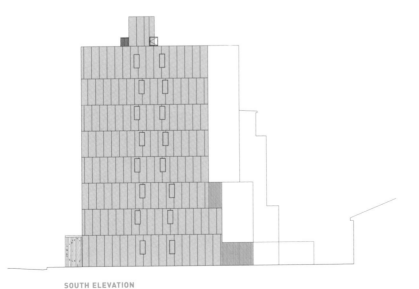

SOUTH ELEVATION

Above
West facade from
Fairfield Road.

Left
Looking down on podium.

Opposite
East facade.

5

□ Venice, Italy

Thyssen-Bornemisza Limited Edition Art Pavilion
Island of San Lazzaro degli Armeni, Venice

Francesca von Habsburg

Francesca von Habsburg is the daughter of Hans Heinrich Thyssen-Bornemisza, the founder of the museum of that name in Madrid. She is continuing the family tradition of patronising the arts with a focus on the arts of today. In 2002 she founded T-B A21 which stands for Thyssen-Bornemisza Art for the 21st Century. Based in Vienna, T-B A21 has developed the 'space in progress' concept and uses public spaces and industrial sites to exhibit works from its collection. The Thyssen-Bornemisza Limited Edition Art Pavilions, of which this is the first example, extend this programme by presenting works of art in individual temporary pavilions instead of monolithic environments.

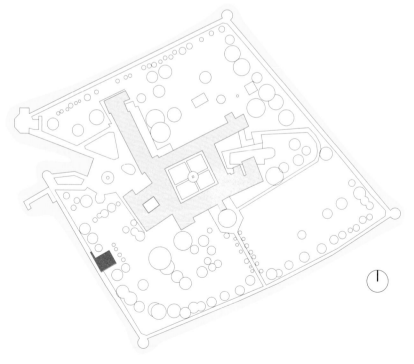

SITE PLAN

Comb, Ghana
A disc, a square and a screen within an everyday object.

Area Schedule

Gallery 175m²	
Loggia 54m²	
Ramped Access 28m²	

Total Area 257m²

This pavilion is conceived as a two-sided belvedere: a pathway leads to a loggia from which there is a dramatic view of the laguna or, in the other direction, access to an impressive art work by the Islandic artist Olafur Eliasson. As it is constructed of prefabricated components, it is capable of being moved to another location. With the use of a fork-lift truck for the heavier components, the work of erecting and demounting the pavilion is planned to take a team of around eight people 7–10 days and 5 days respectively. For economy, lightness, and the ease of replacing damaged components, timber and timber products are the primary materials used in its construction. The colour of the bituminous cladding corresponds with the colour of the interior.

Materials

Bituminous
fibre board

Orientated
strand board

Heat treated
timber

Site Concept

Position

The site is located between two trees on the island of San Lazzaro and overlooks the laguna.

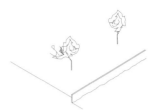

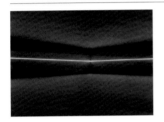

Access

From the direction of the vaporetto stop, a pathway and a sequence of three ramps lead into the pavilion.

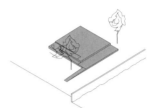

Enclosure

The main volume is constructed in timber and encloses a column-free space.

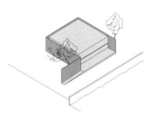

Protection

The external walls of the timber enclosure are protected from the weather by sheets of corrugated bituminous fibre.

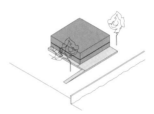

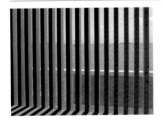

Louvres

The louvres protect the entrance sequence from the glare-inducing view across the laguna and provide an opportunity for the eye to adjust to the light levels inside and outside the pavilion.

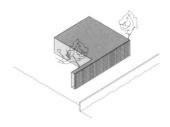

The Venice pavilion was specifically designed to present *Your black horizon*, an installation by the artist Olafur Eliasson commissioned by T-BA 21. In the windowless main space, a horizontal line at eye level serves as the primary light source. Located in a slot in the construction of each wall, the light slowly changes colour every 15 minutes and moves through the spectrum of the Venetian sky as filmed on a single day. By means of the ramp, the space is entered without disrupting the horizon line. While standing in the space the human eye is unable to see any of the construction details of the interior and, for this reason, *Your black horizon* is about personal orientation in both inner and outer space.

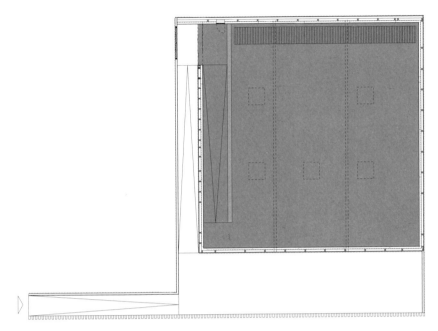

PLAN

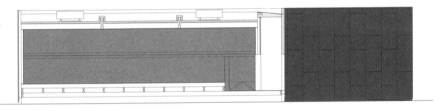

SECTION LOOKING WEST

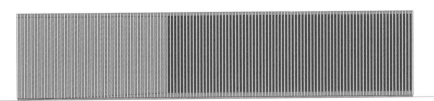

WEST ELEVATION

Above
The timber screen.

Left
Pavilion looking across
the laguna.

Left
Side view and entrance.
Rear of pavilion showing
bituminous cladding.

Opposite
Entrance ramp.

Above
End wall of Loggia.

Left
View through timber
screen.

Left
View of internal ramp.

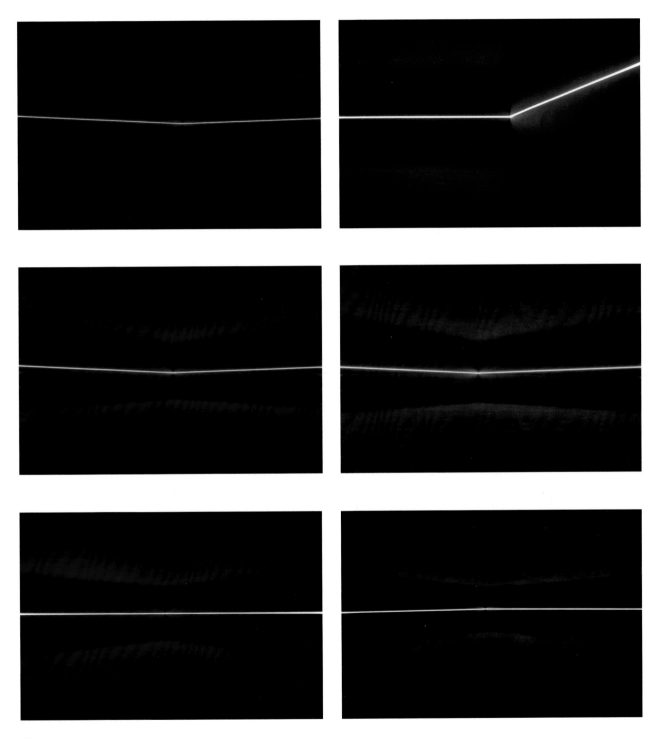

Your black horizon, 2005
Olafur Eliasson

Above
View of exit ramp
and screen.

Opposite
Loggia and exit ramp.

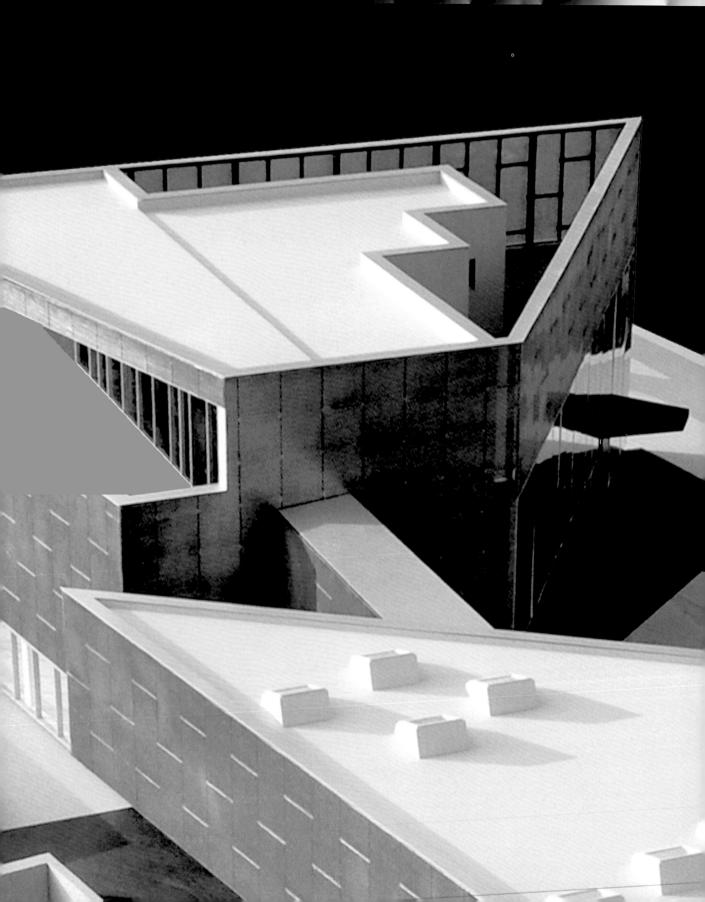

6

L O N D O N

□ **Deptford**

S O U T H W A R K

Stephen Lawrence Centre
Brookmill Road, Deptford

Stephen Lawrence Center, 2004–2007

Stephen Lawrence, 1974–1993

Stephen Lawrence was a young black man who was dedicated to becoming an architect and improving the condition of Britain's inner cities. In 1993, he was brutally murdered. The Stephen Lawrence Trust was established in 1998 with a remit to invest in young people whose life-chances are constrained by hardship, to broaden access to the creative professions, and to promote equality, diversity and social cohesion. Located in South East London, the Stephen Lawrence Centre is intended to make Stephen's dream an accessible reality for disadvantaged young people in the area where he lived.

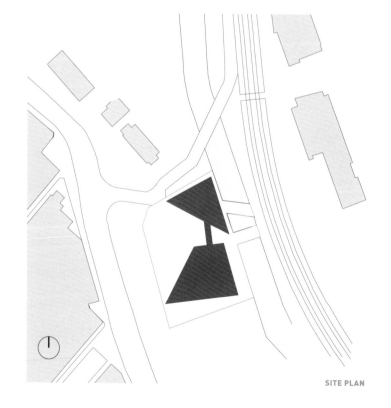

SITE PLAN

Gold dust boxes, Ghana
Two sizes of casket, one raised, with decorated lids.

The site has a small river to the east and a neighbourhood park to the south. It is located between two types of housing: traditional terraced houses to the west and a line of higher apartment buildings to the east. The form and materiality of the centre attempt to reconcile these contrasting conditions within a single development. The height of the main volumes continues the scale of the terraced housing, whilst the use of powder-coated expanded steel sheet as a cladding material is intended to continue the light-responsive quality of the foliage in the park.

Area Schedule

Core and circulation 490m²
Classrooms 225m²
Exhibition 100m²
Creative Arts Lab 85m²
Plant and services 80m²
Administration 80m²
Common Space 75m²
Art Studio 75m²
Mentoring Program 50m²
Business Support Facility 40m²
IT Resources Spaces 20m²

Total Area 1320m²

Materials

| Expanded metal mesh | Glass panels by Chris Ofili | Wood wool | Pressure treated timber soft wood | Red rubber flooring | Polished concrete | Polycarbonate | Sundeala |

Site Concept

Volume

If the site were developed with a sold volume, it would form a barrier between the road and the river.

External space

To provide a route from the road to the river, the volume has been divided into two blocks. The front faces of each block are aligned with two of the main approaches and define a forecourt.

Separate blocks

To increase the visibility of the river, the smaller block is lifted off the ground. The larger block has terraces at roof level.

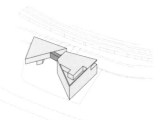

Bridge

As the facilities in the two blocks may need to be used together, they have been connected at first floor level by an enclosed bridge.

Ground plane

The design of the ground plane is based on a drawing by the artist Chris Ofili. It is intended to encourage young people to enter the site and make use of the centre.

The larger building has an entrance space which occupies the full width of the west facade while the remaining spaces are mainly used for IT teaching. Complementing its neighbour, the smaller building contains two studio spaces and several sound rooms. Ease of access is a critical issue and the open forecourt, the gap between the buildings, and the elevated position of the smaller building establish a highly porous relationship between the centre and its surroundings. Two footbridges cross the river and provide access to a rejuvenated ecological and wildlife corridor alongside the Ravensbourne River.

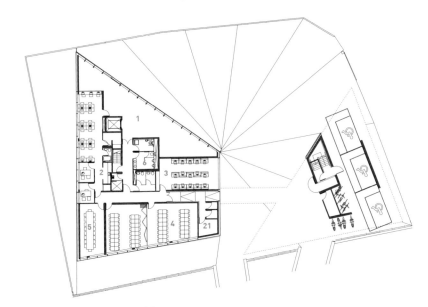

GROUND-FLOOR PLAN

FIRST-FLOOR PLAN

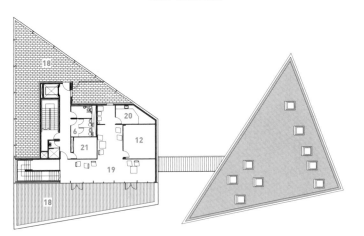

SECOND-FLOOR PLAN

1 Foyer
2 Office
3 Business development
  suite
4 Classroom
5 Meeting room
6 WC
7 Teenage IT room
8 IT Hub
9 Adults IT
10 Mentor room

11 Art studio
12 Storage
13 Local radio
14 Video editing
15 Music mixing room
16 Gallery control
17 Studio
18 Terrace
19 Common room
20 Kitchen
21 Services

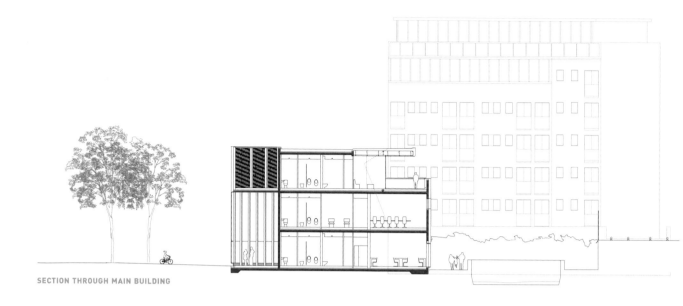

From the main building, there are excellent views in all directions. The two-storey entrance space looks out across the forecourt, with the angled columns forming an architectural screen. The main teaching spaces have views of the park or the river and the common room and terrace enjoy similar views at roof level. A second terrace is completely enclosed by screen walls but open to the sky. In the smaller building, the studio spaces and sound rooms are lit by rooflights. The pattern on the entrance facade is based on a drawing by Chris Ofili of a *moiré* pattern. The drawing is printed on a reflective film and laminated between the glass of the curtain walling system. Both buildings have a concrete structure and the internal and external walls make use of dry wall construction.

SECTION THROUGH STUDIO BUILDING

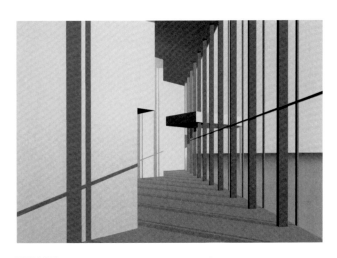

ENTRANCE

DECK

BRIDGE

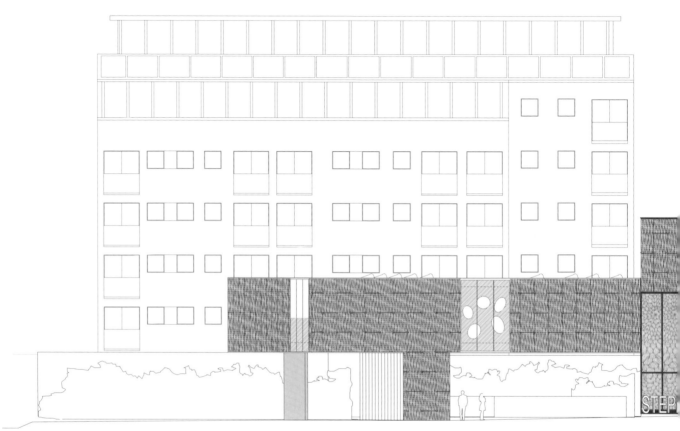

WEST ELEVATION

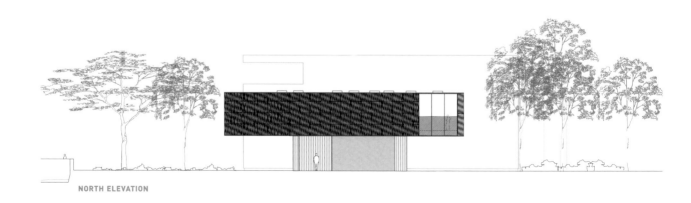

NORTH ELEVATION

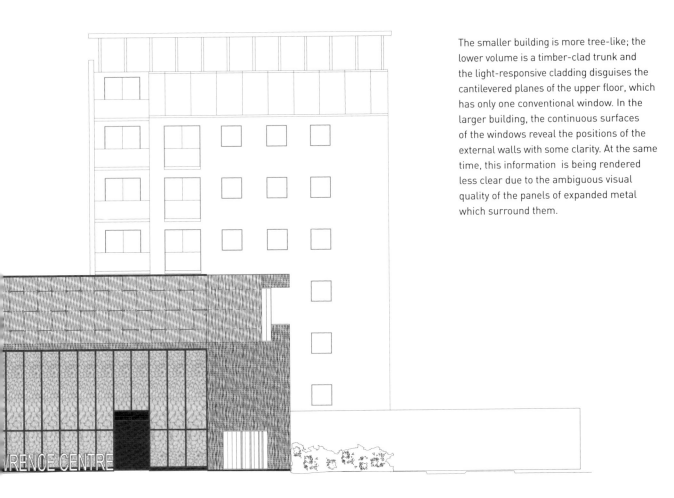

The smaller building is more tree-like; the lower volume is a timber-clad trunk and the light-responsive cladding disguises the cantilevered planes of the upper floor, which has only one conventional window. In the larger building, the continuous surfaces of the windows reveal the positions of the external walls with some clarity. At the same time, this information is being rendered less clear due to the ambiguous visual quality of the panels of expanded metal which surround them.

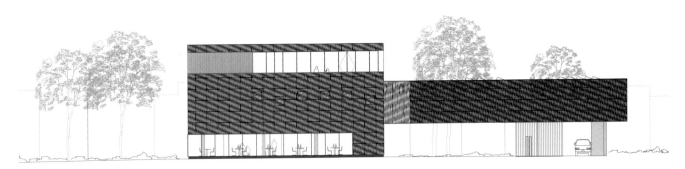

EAST ELEVATION

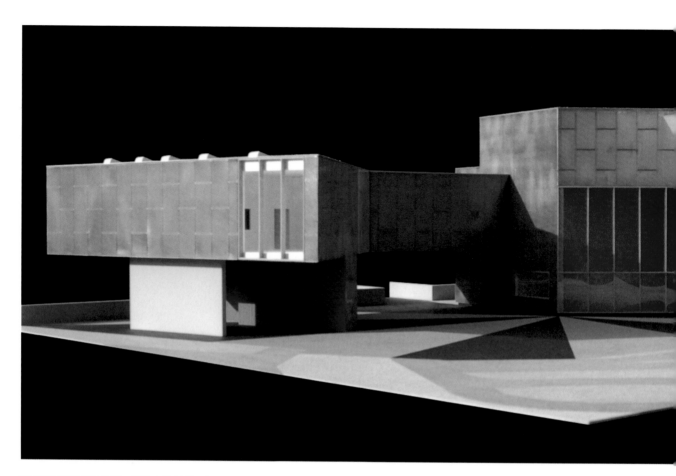

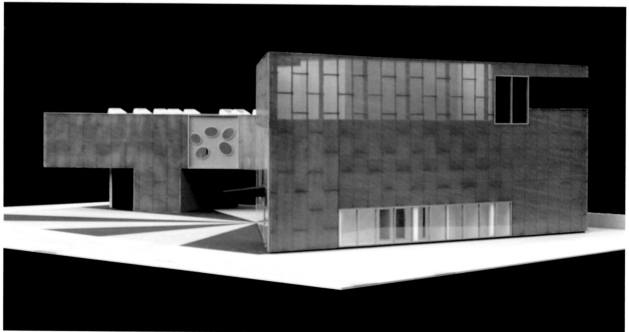

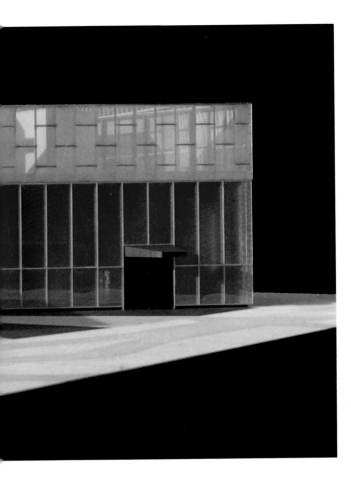

Left
Forecourt and main
entrance.

Below
East facade and roof
terraces.
Studio block and bridge.

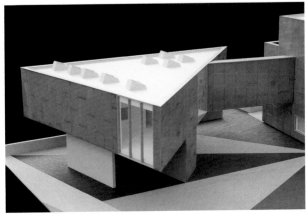

Opposite
Forecourt and
south facade.

OMITTING THE VOID: AN ARCHITECTURE OF ENGAGEMENT

PETER ALLISON IN CONVERSATION WITH DAVID ADJAYE

PETER ALLISON: Since setting up Adjaye/Associates in 2000, your practice has expanded and taken on a broad range of projects from artistic collaborations to affordable housing and major public buildings. Could you say something about your concept for the office as an organisation and how you would like it to be understood by a wider public.[1]

DAVID ADJAYE: Adjaye/Associates is the umbrella for a variety of productions. I am very interested in the word 'productions' as the operative that explains what we do. It is really a structure to allow me to deliver at a series of scales: specific ideas in a range of locations.

PA: There seems to be a move towards an urban scale in the recent work.

DA: The office is an organism that learns through rehearsal, as I call it, and, as it grows through rehearsal, it expands. It has been a growth through a series of small, to medium, to now large projects. The hope is that, as we go through the gates at each stage, we are able to work on a richer cross section of scales. It is very interesting at the moment, especially the larger scale.

PA: Is the range of projects that you are involved with part of a strategy which, at a time when the position of architects seems to be under threat, is intended to show how architecture can make a substantial contribution in many different situations?

DA: I think that architecture has been shoehorned into a position where it is identified as a specific kind of product and the public perceive the profession as glorified stylists. The element of spatial invention is missing and what I am trying to say through the work is that architecture has to try and grasp the whole picture again.

PA: Does your use of the word 'production' imply a degree of collaboration in the development process?

DA: When you make public buildings, it is incumbent on you to understand what the requirements are within the communities and the specific groups that are being targeted. We do not do that on our own, we form teams in order to get that information. When it is about what I call 'soft information', gathering consensus information through workshops and playing out different scenarios, we work with urbanists and sociologists. Working in the margins requires the kind of expertise that the bureaucrats do not have and the architect is brought in as a kind of front-line soldier, a catalyst, to discover issues which may be latent and have not come up to the surface.

PA: Would that apply to the Stephen Lawrence Centre?

DA: Yes. Stephen Lawrence was about very intimate discussions with a new body that is trying to identify its future role, its own trajectory, and is trying to understand how it positions itself within communities.

PA: In this context, how does the organisation of the office reflect your agenda and your overall intentions?

DA: The structure of the office is set up to enable things to be made. My job is to ensure that the information which is collected is focussed into a precise conceptual frame that then delivers the built idea. Each project is managed by a director. I try to keep my distance from the design teams so that I can concentrate on the essential components of the strategy.

PA: One thing which distinguishes your work is the way in which it combines technical innovation, in the use of materials for instance, with an awareness of the formal possibilities demonstrated by the history of modern architecture and the history of architecture in general. Is this bringing together of concerns which are often thought to be mutually exclusive part of your programme?

DA: Yes, only because I cannot conceive of an architecture which does not refer back to a lineage that is already established. I conceive of my work within scenarios that have existed so I am not interested in the idea of architecture as thought out of the bubble, a new architecture for every occasion. I am very interested in making a connection within things that exist. In London, for instance, it is inevitable that one acknowledges what the high-tech world tried to do: the systematisation of architecture, the importance of components, the idea of striving towards a certain kind of quality. The leaders of this movement were also referring to developments in America so there is a larger trajectory. I think that it is imperative to work through that lineage to the other side. But I am not interested in making explicit references: it is much more important to recognise where a position has been taken to and how you move it on. When two things have been put so close to each other that it is perfect, it is imperative for me to look for other possibilities which have not been covered within those developments. If we are talking about how to make things, I am always searching for the potentials that point towards how you add to the discourse by giving the widest range to the issues that are out there.

PA: The high-tech example is interesting because your own work seems to reverse the intentions of high-tech. You use materials in a more raw state and the emphasis is not on the continuity of the system but on making a composition of separate spatial components.

DA: Our work can probably be read as the complete opposite of high-tech but, in my mind, it is the completion of a bigger idea.

PA: I know that you worked in Portugal. Is there something about your experience there that contributed to your own work?

DA: Portugal was instrumental in my understanding of practice. Until I went there, my understanding of how to make buildings was not complete. In London we had moved to a position where the construction industry had become a very dominant force that led the way in which construction was made. Architects were stuck with a limited number of scenarios which had been set up by industry. In Portugal, on the other hand, they were at once in the future but still in the past; there was a moment when a bright architect was able to manipulate those processes. They could see what would happen if they did nothing and they could see the opportunity to shift the diagram. That is Alvaro Siza's greatest achievement: to turn the tanker, the boat, another way and to say there is another way of doing things. He invented a bespoke way of making architecture and turned it into the mainstream way of making architecture. Eduardo Souto de Moura does exactly the same. Portuguese architects have become very skilled in understanding how to work within the construction field, within the environments in which they have a sociological interest.

PA: We have previously discussed the relative advantages of architectural arrangements that are intended to have a strong sense of formality and others which are more informal. Why is it that you think that the more informal option has greater potential?

DA: The history of architecture has demonstrated that the formal has been at the forefront in terms of articulating the aesthetics of architecture but that the informal has always played a powerful role within society. I think that the formal has always been about a way of viewing an ideal whereas the informal is about everyday reality. I feel that since the Renaissance, architecture has run away with this notion of the ideal and has attempted to impose it as the modus operandi. Now that there is an exhaus-tion of this mode, there has been a swing towards the fantastic: the ideal can no longer operate in society so let's make pure fiction, let's make amazing buildings which only have to entertain us. Behind this question is the fact that we know how to deliver formal buildings but we are not so good at making informal those buildings that are about how human beings interact. We need to get a stereo image.

PA: So it is the fusion of the two modes and the ability to manoeuvre between the two.

DA: I think that is the moment when architecture will become relevant to society again.

PA: At the other end of the scale, your public buildings also appear to have a connection with some of the houses that you have designed. Is the possibility of moving between similar formal arrangements, employed at different scales, part of your method?

DA: Yes, ultimately they are even though I deny it and suggest that they are separate mechanisms. They are somehow linked; they are systems that test scenarios but they do this in different ways in each case. The houses are always very important.

PA: As in the houses, the powerful simplicity of the exterior often acts as a veil to a changeful and varied interior. Is the tension between external image and internal reality a significant driver in the public buildings?

DA: Sometimes, by default. It happens as a result of the

analysis and the complexity of the navigation. The issues that I am dealing with are well rehearsed; they do not work as contradictions or switch down the thinking. If they confirm the initial analysis, they can be magnified and really pushed to their ultimate position within the structure that I am given: budget, time and so on.

PA: The Papers on Architecture group, of which you were the youngest member, shunned formal elaboration for its own sake and developed a preference for simple rectangular forms which could be successively modified in response to context, programme and so on. Has this view informed your approach?[2]

DA: I felt that here was a group of people who could have a collective understanding about something fundamental, about the power of abstraction. This power of abstraction that can be applied to something that has been reduced to an elemental state: I think that is the common link between all of us who were involved in the Papers.

PA: Despite a scattering of towers, London is still a horizontal, layered city. The conditions at roof level are different from those at street level and the intermediate levels. Responding to such changes in section provides another basis for sensitising a rectangular form. To what extent is this reflected in your work?

DA: This intuition about the horizontality of London, the layering of London, underscores the nature of the rectangle as the form which is best able to contain the horizontality found in the city.

PA: Are you talking about a platform, a system of decks?

DA: Yes, so there is a play, in almost every project, which is informed by that fundamental notion. The rectangle works brilliantly in the density of the city but as soon as you move into the landscape, the rectangle starts to become problematic. It becomes too much about the architect having a notion of perfection rather than reality.

PA: When you talk about landscape, is there an example that you can refer to?

DA: Stephen Lawrence Centre is sited in a park.

PA: The development of your practice is closely linked with London's East End where your office is located. Have the traditions and urban patterns of the East End informed your view of how to make public buildings?

DA: What I like about the East End is that its Victorian patrons anticipated a landscape which was about making decent homes for its workers but, within this ordering system, the social life of the people led to some very interesting variables. These differences, which operate across the landscape of the East End, are far more explicit in their urban impact than they are in areas where buildings are more closely matched to people's expectations. There is a disconnect here between the unit, basic but decent, and the aspirations of the person living there — which may be much larger than the entire building. I feel very comfortable with this double ambiguity. To understand how to make them into concrete manifestations has been the exercise; to no longer see them as a problem has been the whole rationale of the architecture.

PA: I know that the Idea Stores, both of which are in the East End, are not meant to be seen as traditional libraries and that, in each case, they have been carefully integrated within areas of shopping. Nevertheless, they cannot be confused with retail buildings. Their appearance suggests a new type of institution but one which has the accessibility of a shop. How did you maintain the idea of a public building whilst addressing the requirement for open access?

DA: That was the challenge: to avoid stylistic caricature and answer the question on what a public building should be about now. At a philosophical level, it can be discussed as a series of perceptual scenarios, a series of experiences which come together into a narrative, describing a certain kind of journey. That reading brings something into the contemporary for me: being able to read those scenarios. With that in mind, the question of shopping or not shopping is not an issue. It is subsumed within the notion of experience: spatial experiences, how they are curated and how they are made. In parallel, there are notions about porosity, accessibility and symbolism that play within public buildings. It is one place where the iconography of the architecture can be quite overt in order to clarify what is to be done and what is not to be done, what is civil and what is not, what is right, what is wrong. They need to be clear for a new user group operating within a specific environment and that is what interests me: understanding what happens within the larger context that the public building creates.

PA: The narrative as an accessible experience but you also used the word 'iconography'?

DA: It is highly abstracted but it is still legible, and I am very interested in this kind of duality. By operating at both ends of the scale, I hope to allow for a wide range of possible responses. I have to be aware, even when I reduce completely, that I am still making form and ultimately form has a kind of presence and a psychological impact on its user no matter how reduced it might be. Even though I might be working with a notion of abstraction, I am aware that certain motifs within that abstraction have cognitive recognition within the public realm. At the same time, I am manipulating my own view of these abstractions to talk about new ways of perceiving various codes concerning how you make things available or not available. In Whitechapel, the notion of porosity was extremely important. The Sainsbury supermarket, which

PETER ALLISON AND DAVID ADJAYE 123

is behind it, is incredibly ordered and much more like the traditional idea of a public building. Overall, it is a dumb block with a porch and there is even an arcade that leads you to the porch. In my building, in contrast, I picked up a more pluralistic reading of the urban situation. The Whitechapel building, because of the way it is organised, is about several buildings that make one condition. The porosity is no longer that of a portico that you enter to discover the delights or edifying issues that are inside but concerns a multiplicity of access which allows you to discover your own personal journey through something that is about publicness.

PA: Moving on to questions of perception, in the art installations that you have designed in collaboration with the painter Chris Ofili, the boundary between architecture and art is unclear and one's awareness moves freely between these two areas without the self-consciousness that normally informs this kind of situation.[3] In your public buildings, where your design responds closely to many aspects of the context, is it your intention to produce a similar response?

DA: Yes, when I work with an artist, or working with Chris specifically, what became clear was an aspiration on both sides to give up to the work and to try and allow the totality of the work to somehow drive us rather than the other way round. The ambition was to reconcile some things that had become irreconcilable through the history of art, as art finally disconnected itself from the built environment and became abstract. It was an attempt to bring the discourse together again, not for any romantic reasons but to talk about the Janus-like relationship that they have with each other and to form a whole. The experience of the whole is a sensation that can never be attributed to the object or the subject, space being the subject for me. What this taught me, in terms of how to make public buildings, was that in allowing the collage of the systems to impact the production, you

were able to deliver a certain kind of richness. I don't mean that there are lots of hands, but that the authoring process of different systems are then curated under one umbrella: social analysis, engineering and so on.

PA: So the perceptual boundaries to the project become very indistinct and extend out into the context at different scales. To continue with the Ofili connection, in his paintings, the seductive detail of the surface engages the eye before the mind has time to take in the structure of the composition, which provides the pretext for the surface treatment itself. The usual formalities that go with looking at paintings are swiftly put to one side. Was this part of your thinking in your collaboration with Ofili on the design of the facade of the Stephen Lawrence Centre?

DA: Stephen Lawrence is an attempt to play the same exercise on an urban scale. Not to play it as a sort of game but to really present the notion of a perceptual plane as the introduction to a piece of public architecture.

PA: Having been seduced into the space of an Ofili painting by its surface qualities, you discover that the underlying composition is quite monumental and a dialogue is immediately set up between the formality of the composition and the fluidity of the surface. Is there a similar polarisation in your projects?

DA: Stephen Lawrence is probably the project where this plays out in a very direct way, like Chris' paintings. Stephen Lawrence is about the invention of a new institution which aims to engage the public in a very big debate, without necessarily trumpeting the debate upon first perception of the building. Its remit is to bring you into the discourse without hammering it over you. The space that acts as the interface between the engine of the building, as it were, and the point where the people of the building encounter the public is a monumental one. A lot of people have asked me why it is so big, what its importance is and

The Upper Room, 2002 by Chris Ofili; designed by David Adjaye.

why it is not just a sweet little space that people can meet in. For me, it is because this is one building where I wanted a formal order, a formal scenario: it is a formal building. But knowing that a formal building would be the reverse of what this place would want to be, because it would counter everything that they set out to do, the formality is set up as a play that you trip into.

PA: It is an oblique for of monumentality.

DA: Yes, it is an informal version of monumentality.

PA: A final point on Ofili's paintings: whilst referring to various aspects of contemporary culture, he is able to give a new and wider relevance to a traditional subject,

the human figure. Is there an element in your work of wishing to revalidate certain aspects of architecture?

DA: I think that the project is about the revalidation of architecture in public life, not the negation of it. This is about trying to bring architecture back to its civic position within culture and not to relegate it to that of spectacle and entertainment, which it is fast becoming.

PA: Besides the vertical core and changeful exterior, there is the question of interior space. You seem to put the emphasis on spatial continuity, creating an architectural landscape with continuous shifts in scale and orientation. Compared with the other arts, is the spatial element where architecture comes into its own?

DA: Absolutely, the spatial fluidity encapsulates a certain contemporariness that we have now. It is synonymous with our perception. I think that space is perceived in an evolutionary way, in the same way that language and other things are understood. We perceive space through spatially choreographed narratives now. I am actually talking about cinematic space and the notion of curating a scenography through architecture is profoundly important to understanding how you make things happen. The fluidity, and the cut or the edit between one space and the other, and how they continue each other, is supremely important. It is an old word, threshold, but, for me, it is the joining.

PA: Curiously, you often seem to omit the threshold, or perhaps the whole building has become a threshold.

DA: Yes, because it is one thing. The only way I can explain that is to talk about the fluidity of a film, where there are thresholds every minute but one continuous system. The threshold is no longer necessary.

PA: Many of your public buildings include a space which is not strictly speaking necessary for functional reasons. I am thinking of the multi-storey entrance in the Whitechapel Idea Store, the step-shaped lobby at the Stephen Lawrence Centre, the multi-storey slot between the two halves of the Fairfield Road housing project. They serve to anchor the design in its location and they contribute enormously to the identity of each project. Do you conceive of these spaces at an early stage in the design process or do they emerge as the rest of the project takes shape?

DA: I have to admit that they are conceived at the beginning, which sounds contrary to the process that I have been describing. There is a certain amount of investigation that I make personally about a project, almost, as it were, in silence. Later, when I gather more information, it is a real test of the resilience of that silent perception. There seems to be a strategic decision about omitting the void, as I call it, which has to occur within every project. The creation of that void really determines the rest of the scenario that the project will take. Once that void is established, and its significance understood in the realm of the project, it acts as an anchor mechanism to drive the development of the design right through to completion.

PA: Strictly speaking, such voids are not necessary but they hold everything together and the fact that they are easy to understand, and to appreciate and enjoy, means that they become the space that summarises and represents the project in its entirety. It seems to me that these spaces help to make the architecture accessible and without it the projects would not be so inclusive.

DA: Absolutely, they would be completely abstract.

PA: When the overall organisation of each of your public buildings is extremely sensitive to its surroundings, it seems paradoxical that through these additional spaces you are able to add something to each location of which there was little trace before your intervention.

DA: The ambition is to do that and I do not consider a project is successful until that operation has occurred. The project does not even start until that operation is discovered on each site. I am not able to work until that discovery is made.

PA: And this comes out of the research processes that you were talking about earlier on.

DA: There is an intuition which starts it and then an underpinning which comes through the analysis.

PA: So the intuition also guides the analysis.

DA: Yes, although I never reveal the intuition to my directors until the information is fully gathered. I am not interested in reinforcing my own conceit about something. I am more interested in seeing how close it can come to satisfying the complete scenario. I have to allow the information to impact completely on the concept that I have set up intuitively, without defending it.

PA: Your designs also include spaces whose main purpose is for people to hang out in: the front-of-house space at Stephen Lawrence, for instance. Are these spaces intended to blur the traditional idea of what constitutes a public building?

DA: I am very interested in effects that occur in paintings which just depict the image of the city with its people in one scenography. It allows us to understand architecture as the basis for making the abstraction of place more coherent. So, yes, I am always making these public rooms, as it were, which are not really about the articulation of the architecture but about a way in which the architecture steps back in order to make these places.

PA: Are you saying that the element of abstraction, in relation to what is there, is an important attribute of these spaces?

DA: Yes. On the rear of the Whitechapel Idea Store, for instance, where the pavilion completes the composition of rearness and makes a kind of public square, with all the potential backs and the not-so-formal fronts that were in that large enclosure, of which the car park is just one component. That formality is really interesting to me: it is not quite a representational moment, it is the way in which the building activates a certain kind of abstractness into something which is not abstract. By its position and its scale, or motif or suggestion, the building makes sense of something that was always there but was never seen to make sense in any kind of representa-

tional way that we previously understood. In Stephen Lawrence there is another move occurring: I am picking up on one of the axial roads and making a quadrant, anchoring the corner. The triangle becomes a negative cut-out which makes an informal public room held before the park, and then the park is allowed to happen after the threshold of the square.

PA: An informal public room in a landscape situation.

DA: Which cannot have the formal properties of a set composition.

PA: And becomes a place for people to spend time.

DA: Yes, because I think that they instinctively understand this scenario.

PA: Due to your father's work, your family lived in several countries when you were a child. Did you have an interest in architecture at this time and, in particular, were you aware of the contribution which public buildings make to the environment?

DA: Yes, but I was not aware of it in a very conscious way. I was aware of it as a way of understanding differences between cultures. What became very clear was having to negotiate different notions of publicness, different notions of privateness, different notions of civicness, by shifting through many places in probably the most formative time of my upbringing. That had a subliminal effect which later became triggered as a desire to work within this world. There is no doubt that there is a link between the two.

PA: I know that as part of your own teaching you have encouraged students to include a public dimension in projects which might be expected to be rather self-contained, such as film studios. Is this type of hybridisation part of your approach?

DA: Hybridisation is the word I have been using for a while and I have only recently moved it to 'imbrication'. Hybridisation somehow implies that I am making something new whereas what I am talking about is much more to do with overlapping, reliance by overlapping — almost like tiles. I am interested in that ability to prop things against each other or around each other to make perceptions of multiplicity. This is something that I have understood and that is really at the heart of what I am trying to do. The word that I have found, imbrication, is a sociologists' term.

PA: Are the shifts in identity which result from this process a significant attribute of what you are doing: that you can see things as having several possible identities?

DA: That, for me, is part of the experience of the whole thing but it is not meant to be understood as made up of singular systems. There is overlap and the overlap is where the blurring occurs, the editing occurs. From one tile to the other, as it were, you do not sense that you are moving through two different systems; you feel like you are going through one continuous system. I believe that what I am trying to do is not say that the subject, architecture, is made anew but that it has more layers to it. That is its evolution.

PA: When I visit your buildings, I have a strong sense that there is a rhythmic connection between different spaces and between details and the whole. Is this type of organisation, where the parts have a synchronic relationship with each other, what you have to identify in the first stages of a design?

DA: This is one of the fundamental pillars of the thinking, that this duality has to occur.

PA: The way in which you use materials can be seen as a graphic representation of the underlying programme of each project, a kind of portrait carried out in the manner of a Cubist collage. Do you see the identity of a project as fixed or is there the possibility of change?

DA: I think that the identity of a project is fixed in time but inherent within that fixing is the possibility of change. The change obviously works within a certain range and, if the elasticity of what is required goes past that range, it is no longer flexible. The potential of what I am prop-osing is not very flexible in the technological sense. They are very specific buildings, they do certain things and work within specific ranges. I feel that, within the speed at which we work in society, the notion that you make more and more flexible containers is actually not working for architecture. For me, it is more interesting to try and find, within the time that we live in, scenarios that have a certain fixity to them, which have a certain specificity which says that they are almost frozen moments of what is possible within this time line.

PA: Your use of materials is marked by a lightness of touch and an immediacy which give a feeling of spontaneity and warmth. Is the appearance of these qualities in your work a result of new materials and construction techniques?

DA: I think it is, that is what we explore. It is ironic that some people think that, because of the newness and the non-hierarchical perception of the materials, I am able to say it can be cheese today, it can be tuna tomorrow, or paper. Actually, it is about a very specific ordering of materials, a very particular ensemble of materials, which speak to what the material is about, speak to the type of project it is. Within the structure of the thing, once you understand the proposal and what is being said, each material plays its correct part within the scenography of the whole.

PA: Do the inspirational images, and their meaning for your work, represent an attempt to extend the iconography of your buildings beyond the normal limits?

DA: Yes, definitely.

PA: Your projects often set up relationships between polarised phenomena, public/private, open/closed, transparent/opaque and so on. Does this pattern come from your intuitions or is it part of a more self-conscious intellectual position?

DA: It is both, really. It is generated from certain intuitive speculations but it is absolutely tested through research and through the production of making buildings in order to establish an objectivity that then defines the project.

PA: Many aspects of your work can be seen as a sustained attempt to increase the accessibility of architecture. With its bold outline, dramatic views, and atmospheric interiors, the Whitechapel Idea Store provides many routes for people from different backgrounds to appreciate and enjoy this extraordinary new facility. Do you see this possibility as a significant issue for contemporary architecture?

DA: I think it is the most important issue in contemporary architecture. In a world where the scenography of the global is on our doorstep, it is no longer possible to sustain a certain kind of enclosed identity. By default, we are all now travellers, either through our televisions or through physical space. The multiplicity of our perception is now a reality of our everyday lives. That profoundly effects the operating mode in which we perceive things: it is no longer singular, in a collective sense. It is no longer about understanding exactly what a certain material does within a space. That does not register with me in the way that it used to, it no longer rises to the challenge of knowledge that has occurred.

That is the game: to match the abilities that we have gained, through time, to get to where we are and to the way in which we perceive space now.

PA: In the context of social inclusion.

DA: Yes, that is the default.

Notes

1. This is an edited version of a conversation that took place at the Adjaye/Associates office on 14 September 2005.

2. The group included Stephen Bates, Adam Caruso, Tony Fretton, Brad Lachore, Mark Pimlott, Juan Salgado, Irénée Scalbert and Jonathan Sergison, and met regularly between October 1994 and November 1995.

3. These include The Upper Room, Victoria Miro Gallery, London, 2002, and within reach, The British Pavilion, Art Biennale, Venice, 2003. The Upper Room was installed at Tate Britain, London, in 2005.

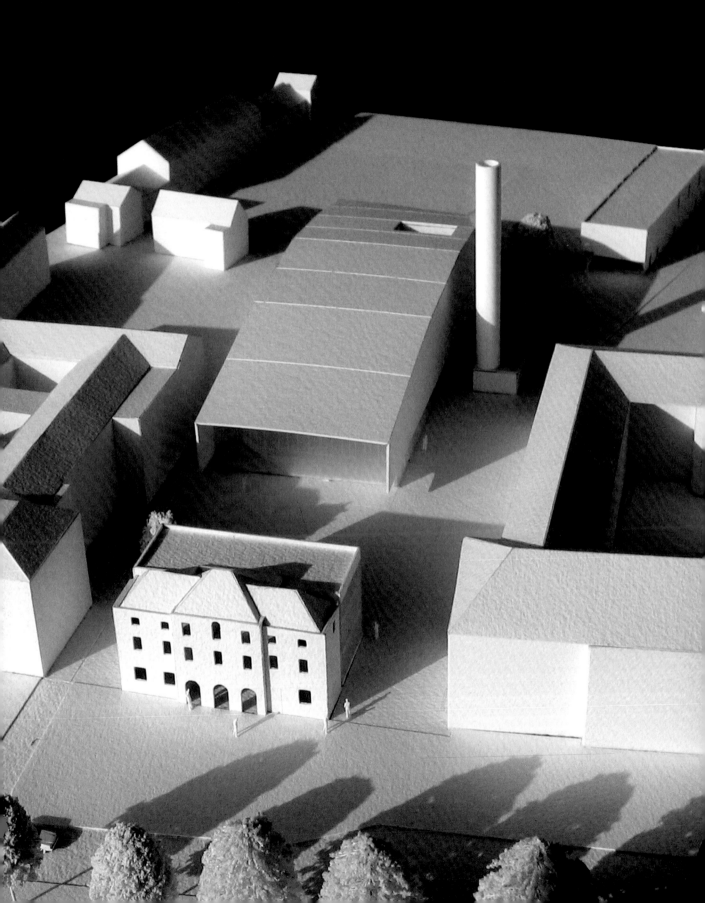

7

HARINGEY

□ **Tottenham**

LONDON

Bernie Grant Arts Centre
Clyde Road Depot, Town Hall Approach Road, Tottenham

Bernie Grant Arts Centre, 2002–2007

Bernie Grant, 1944–2000

The client for this project is the Bernie Grant Centre Partnership, an organisation with joint representation from the Bernie Grant Trust and Haringey Council. The Trust was established in 2000 to continue the work of the UK's first black Member of Parliament. At the heart of their programme is the intention to build social capital, community cohesion and to develop strategies to tackle institutional racism. It was Bernie Grant's view that the Tottenham area had produced a significant number of actors, musicians and writers, and it is for this reason that the trust took the decision to build a performance centre. It is intended to embody the educational aims of the trust and to commemorate Bernie Grant himself.

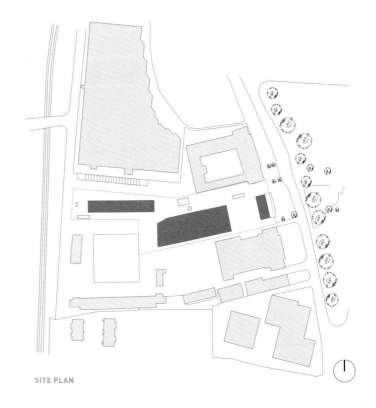

SITE PLAN

Straw-thread mat, Rwanda
A continuous pattern distorted by its materiality.

There are two main elements in this project: the auditorium, which is the focus and *raison d'être* of the entire development, and the other buildings whose purpose is to modify the existing environment in order to provide a suitable setting for the auditorium. The choice of materials reflects this distinction, with the purpleheart and heat-treated timber being used for the interior and foyer of the auditorium building, and the materiality of the other buildings working to support the form and colour of the auditorium.

Area Schedule

Performance Theatre 2450m²
(Auditorium 490m², Back of House 1040m²,
Rehearsal Space 100m², Public Facilities 440m²,
Circulation 340m², Offices 40m²)

Enterprise 855m²
(Enterprise Units 420m², Rehearsal Space 70m²,
Public Facilities 75m², Back of House 90m²,
Circulation 200m²)

Administration 720m²
(Classrooms 150m², Public Facilities 235m²,
Offices 170, Back of House 35m², Circulation 130m²)

Total Area 4025m²

Materials

Purpleheart wood

Heat treated timber

Grey slate

Anodised aluminium

Sienna slate

Metal ridgidal

Grey/green slate

Mastic asphalt

Site Concept

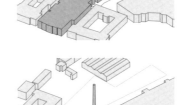

Existing Site

The site was previously occupied by a public baths building. The town hall, to the south, and the college, to the north, are listed buildings.

Demolished Site

The site has been cleared with the exception of the front section of the baths building and the chimney. The facade of the baths building forms part of the historic frontage on Tottenham Green and is also listed. The chimney is a local landmark.

Site Potential

An envelope which follows the site boundary, and is the same height as the neighbouring buildings, describes the volume of space which is available for the project.

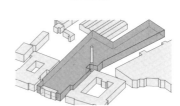

Three Buildings

Each of these buildings represents a significant aspect of the Trust's work and the spaces between them create a porous, campus-type environment which connects with the surrounding area.

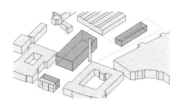

Lowering of Auditorium Roof

This improves the sight lines into the site in positions where the side walls of the auditorium are close to the buildings on either side of the site.

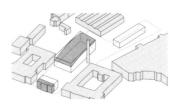

Formal Public Space

Like a triumphal arch, the retained frontage defines an axial route onto the site, leading towards a new public square and the main entrance into the auditorium building. The gaps on each side of the retained frontage frame diagonal views of the site.

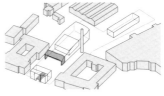

Informal Public Space

At the north-west corner of the auditorium, there is a more informal public space which is used by performers, students, teachers and young business people as they come and go from the stage door of the auditorium and the entrance to the auditorium building.

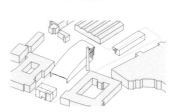

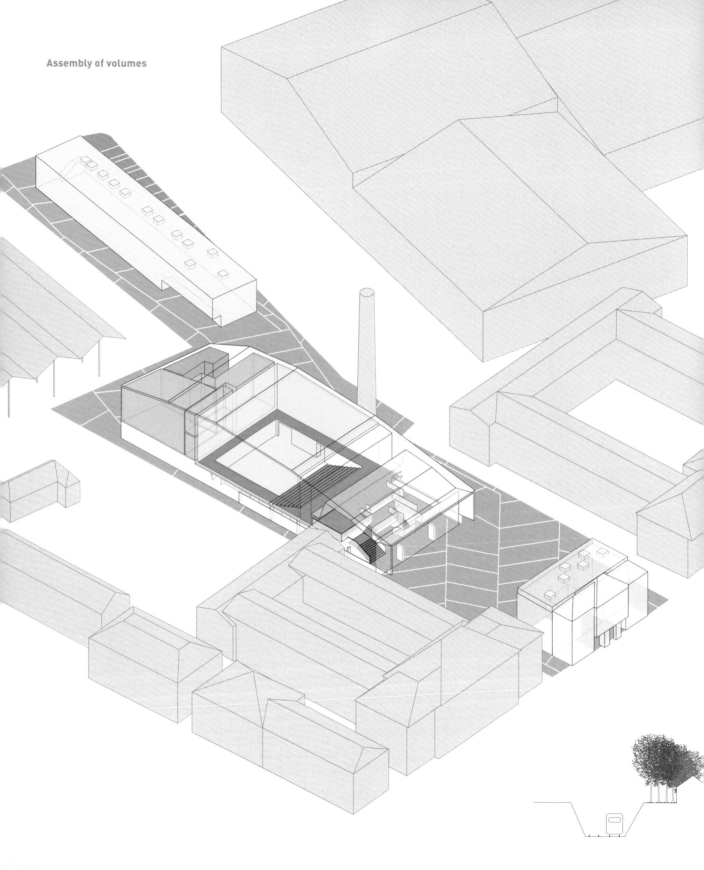

Assembly of volumes

As the site is long and deep, the continuity of the ground plane is maintained by lozenge-shaped plates of asphalt whose diagonal layout leads the eye from one external space to another. The colouring of these plates is graded from green, at the front of the site where it connects with the existing landscaped space, to brown, at the rear of the site where the parking is located. The ground floor of the front building houses the booking office, from which there is direct view of the auditorium itself. The elevations of the new buildings respond to the side walls of the existing buildings. In particular, the back of the front building and the front facade of the auditorium work with the existing walls to form a new civic space whose architectural character complements the landscaped informality of Tottenham Green.

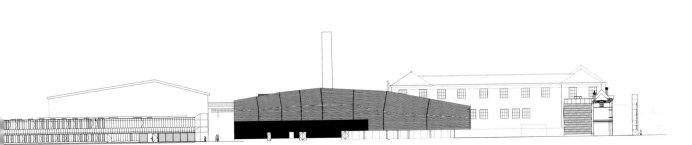

SOUTH ELEVATION

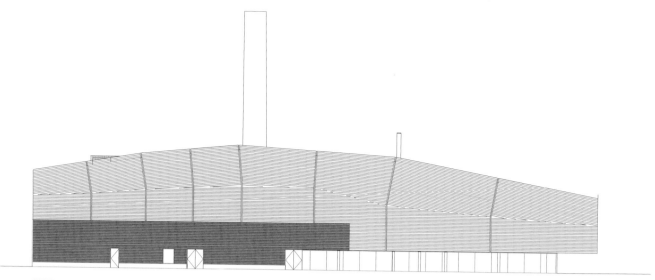

SOUTH ELEVATION

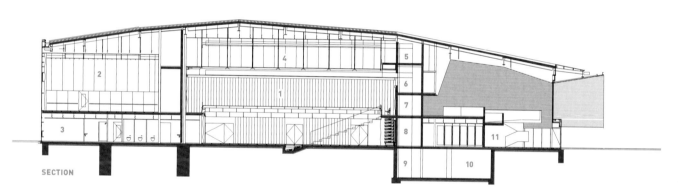

SECTION

1 Auditorium
2 Rehearsal space
3 Changing rooms
4 Lighting gantry
5 Storage
6 Control room

7 WC
8 Corridor
9 Staircase
10 Plant room
11 Entry Foyer

GROUND-FLOOR PLAN

Auditorium

The auditorium includes three main spaces: a foyer and bar, the performance hall and a large rehearsal space, all linked by an efficient circulation system. A tension-wire grid is located above the performance space to provide safe access for lighting control and technical training. The steel structural frame is hidden by the external cladding and the linings of the internal spaces. The roof employs a 'rain-screen' section which is normally used in the construction of external walls.

Guest House, Southern Iraq
Three elevations in one.

EAST ELEVATION

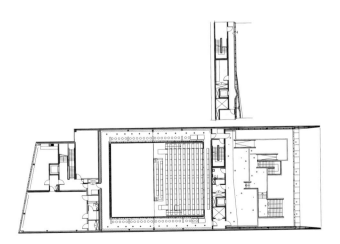

FIRST-FLOOR PLAN

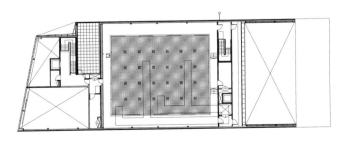

SECOND-FLOOR PLAN

EAST ELEVATION

SOUTH ELEVATION

Front building

The upper floors of the front building are occupied by teaching spaces and small offices. Although the levels are the same throughout, the exterior suggests a Janus-like relationship between the old and new construction. The remaining section of the existing building presents a classically inspired facade, in red brick with stone details, whilst the new construction is clad in grey-black ceramic tiles with a staggered, small-scale grid and no projections beyond the plane of the wall. In the extension, all the window openings are located on the north facade.

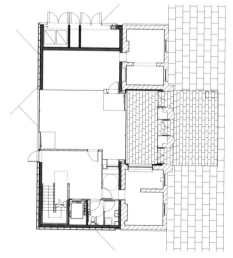

GROUND-FLOOR PLAN

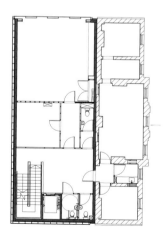

FIRST-FLOOR PLAN

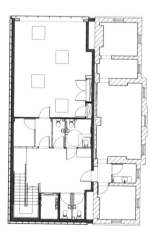

SECOND-FLOOR PLAN

SOUTH ELEVATION

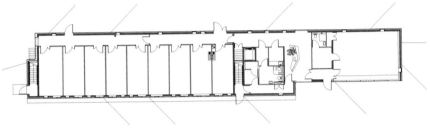

GROUND-FLOOR PLAN

WEST ELEVATION

FIRST-FLOOR PLAN

Enterprise building
This long thin building contains a second rehearsal space, enterprise units for young businesses, and shared support facilities. It is clad with aluminium panels in three different heights that create a sense of ambiguity about the vertical scale. Each of the buildings that make up the Bernie Grant Centre has a steel frame. While in part an economic solution, the cladding and lining of each building is also a direct response to its role within the larger environment of which it is part.

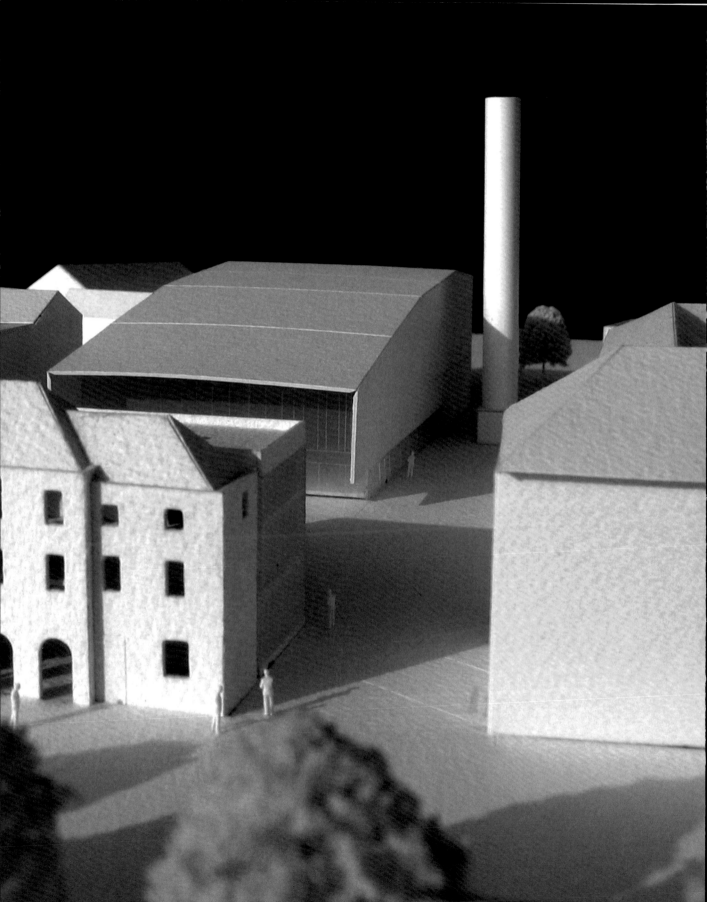

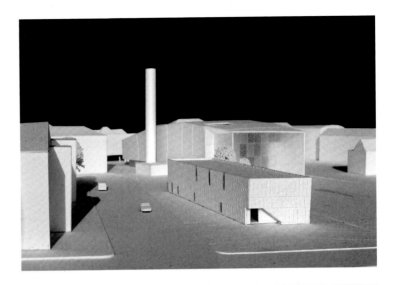

8

UNITED STATES

COLARADO
□ Denver

Museum of Contemporary Art Denver
1275 19th Street, Denver, CO, USA

The Museum of Contemporary Art was founded in 1996 and is currently housed in a renovated fish market in the downtown area. From the beginning it was the intention that Denver should have a world-class facility and, after a selection process which involved six practices participating in a series of public presentations in 2004, Adjaye/Associates were appointed to design a new museum on a site at the corner of a mixed-use block on 15th and Delgany Streets. 15th Street is an important route to and from downtown Denver, to the south-east of the site. Delgany serves the immediate area: there is a metro station to the north of the site and, to the south, it is a short distance to the South Platte River.

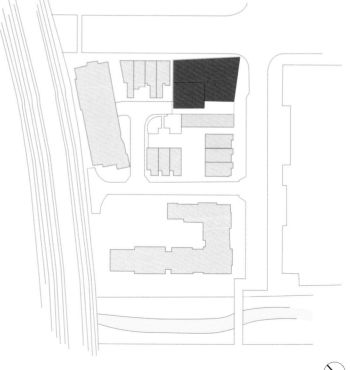

SITE PLAN

roof

Denver MCA
purch. 2006.

still life.

Wooden neck rest, South Africa
An abstract structure which could be a bench or a bridge.

The new building will function on a similar basis to a European kunsthalle and is intended to be 'a place where architecture supports rather than defines the museum's mission'. At any particular time, a range of spaces will be occupied by one or more temporary exhibitions. The major part of the project can be seen as a receptacle whose contents will be subject to considerable variation over the course of time. In order to support this pattern of occupation, the materiality of these areas is based on the use of a limited number of monochromatic materials.

Area Schedule

Atrium/Promonade 380m²
Gallery Space 370m²
Roof Garden 345m²
Ancillary 300m²
Staff Offices 275m²
Circulation 180m²
Informal Gallery Space 145m²
Education 135m²
Restaurant/Members Room 103m²
Reception 50m²
Library 44m²

Total Area 2320m²

Materials

Grey glass   Monopan   Concrete   Tinted concrete   Grey stained redwood

Site Concept

Volume

In keeping with the scale of the neighbouring buildings, the main volume of the new building has a height of four generous storeys.

Facade

In order to establish a visual relationship with the traffic moving into and out of the downtown area, the north-east facade is set at a slight angle to 15th Street.

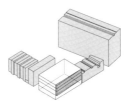

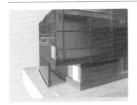

Projection

The south-eastern corner of the building has been pulled forward so that it is visible from the metro station on Delgany.

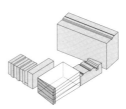

Entrance

This corner is the location of the main entrance onto the site and into the museum.

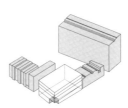

Roof

The members' room and education spaces are housed in separate pavilions which define two sides of a roof terrace.

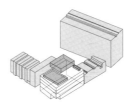

Wall System

The materials selected for the external walls are responsive to the different conditions on each face of the building.

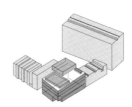

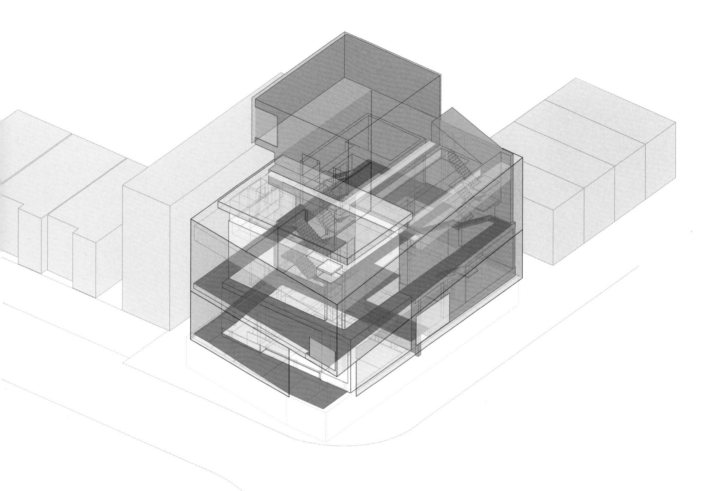

The art spaces are arranged in three separate stacks standing within a larger enclosure. The space between the stacks and the enclosure is used primarily for circulation and the space between the stacks themselves is used to bring natural light into the heart of the building. Two of the stacks support the members' room and the education spaces, and the third one supports an enclosed roof terrace.

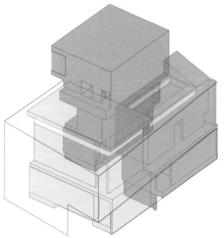

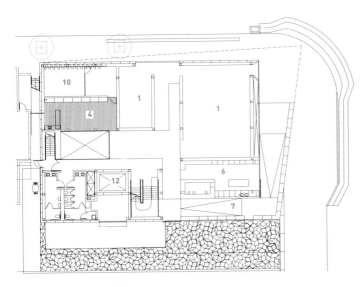

GROUND-FLOOR PLAN

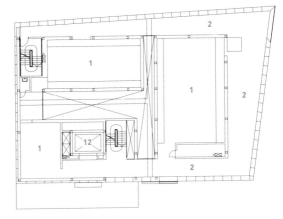

FIRST-FLOOR PLAN

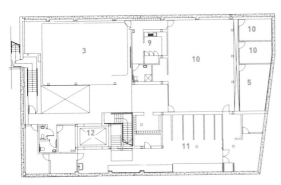

LOWER GROUND-FLOOR PLAN

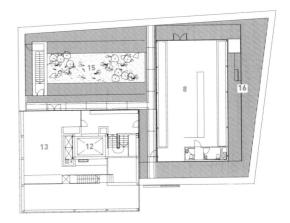

SECOND-FLOOR PLAN

1 Gallery
2 Informal Gallery Space
3 Education Area
4 Library
5 Conference Room
6 Reception
7 Entrance Ramp
8 Restaurant
9 Kitchen
10 Office
11 Art Storage
12 Elevator
13 Kids Room
15 Roof garden
16 Roof terrace

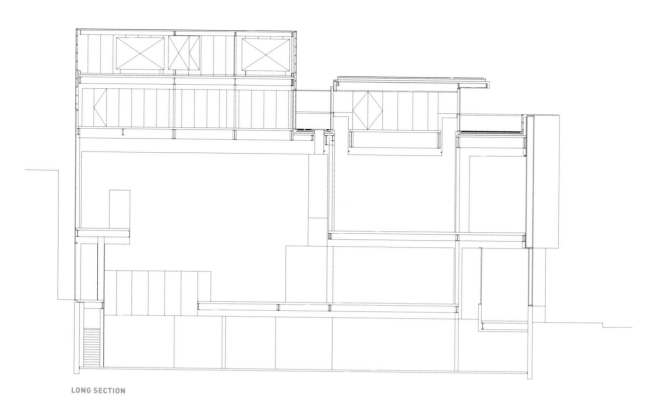

LONG SECTION

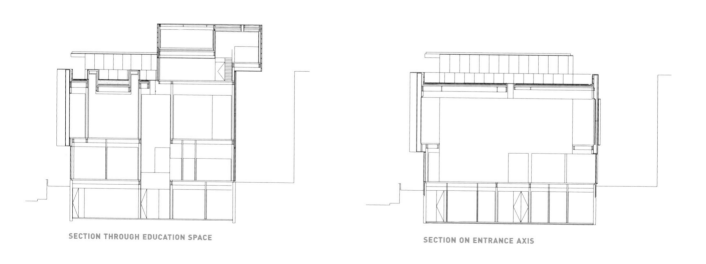

SECTION THROUGH EDUCATION SPACE

SECTION ON ENTRANCE AXIS

In order to accommodate a wide range of art works, the art spaces are differentiated by area and height. The most significant sources of natural light are the T-shaped rooflight and two large windows overlooking the main entrance at the south-east corner of the site. These windows and the rooflight are in positions which derive maximum benefit from direct sunlight throughout the year. The terrace of the members' room and the end wall of the education space enjoy an elevated view of downtown Denver.

SOUTH WEST ELEVATION

NORTH WEST ELEVATION

NORTH EAST ELEVATION

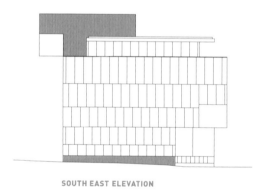

SOUTH EAST ELEVATION

The outer layer of the external walls consists of a double-glazed panel with grey-tinted glass on the outside and clear glass on the inside. The inner faces of both are sandblasted. The inner layer of the wall consists of panels of Monopan, a translucent plastic which provides the required level of thermal insulation. In the gap between the glass and the Monopan, an aluminium frame provides structural support for the panels on either side. The only other cladding material is American Redwood which is stained grey and used at ground and roof levels. On the elevation overlooking the plaza, there is a 6.1m high sliding door to receive extra large items at first floor level.

Views of study model

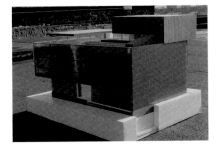

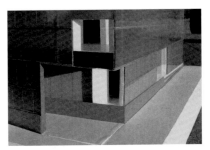

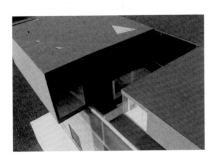

9

TOWER HAMLETS

□ **Poplar**

LONDON

Idea Store Chrisp Street
1 Vesey Path, East India Dock Road, London

The shopping centre at Chrisp Street was built
in the 1950s and serves an area of post-war
housing. At the time it was built, London's docks
were an important source of employment and
the development is connected to the East India
Dock Road by a pedestrian square. The sectional
organisation of the original buildings can be
seen in other examples of the period: the shops
are serviced from vehicular courts and, on
the level above, residential buildings occupy
a series of concrete decks. The site for this
Idea Store consisted of an existing shop unit and
the larger deck which previously formed its roof.

SITE PLAN

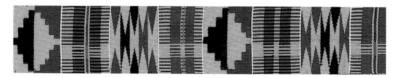

Textile, Ghana
Parallel bars occupied on a rhythmic basis.

Chrisp Street is one in a series of Idea Stores that are intended to encourage local people to make the widest possible use of the facilities provided: a person who starts off by browsing in the audio-visual section may decide to accompany their child to the teen library or, alternatively, sign up for a lifelong-learning class. Whilst sensitive to its location, the exterior of the Chrisp Street Idea Store is perceived as a single volume which can be entered with the minimum of formality and the quality of light and extensive use of timber create a warm and inviting interior. The use of identically coloured glass panels on the two Idea Stores designed by Adjaye/Associates is a large-scale graphic device which reinforces the presence of these facilities within the communities they serve.

Area Schedule

Circulation 180m²
Ancillary 175m²
Classrooms 140m²
Children's Library 125m²
Adult Library 110m²
Surfing Area 95m²
Audio Visual Library 95m²
Cafe 90m²
Teen Library 75m²
Info / Return Books 75m²
Staff Offices 75m²
Exhibition 25m²

Total Area 1260m²

Materials

| Laminated green glass | Laminated blue glass | Laminated clear glass | Laminated veneer lumber | Wood fibre board | Spruce plywood | Powdercoated steel | Perforated steel | Green rubber flooring |

Site Concept

Empty box
The site is on two levels relating to an existing concrete deck. Where necessary the parapets along the edge of the deck have been removed.

Podium floor
The floor area available at deck level is larger than the area at ground level. For this reason, the entrance is organised as a double-height space which links both levels.

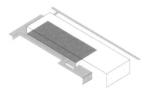

Angled at Front
In order to set up a dynamic relationship with the pedestrian square and East India Dock road, the front facade is set at an angle.

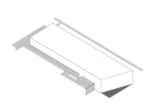

Entrance
The main entrance consists of an automatic sliding door located on the long elevation close to the line at which the two-storey space at ground level becomes a single-storey space on the level above.

Angle at side
To improve the view from the residential building situated to the north of the Idea Store, the corner of the new building has been chamfered off.

Lowered roof
For the same reason, the roof of the new building has been lowered at the north end of the site.

Roof
As it replaces an existing open space, it was important to ensure that the new roof had visual interest when seen from the surrounding buildings. The inclined planes have been finished in different colours and the tops of all the rooflights are at the same level.

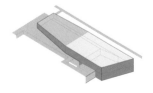

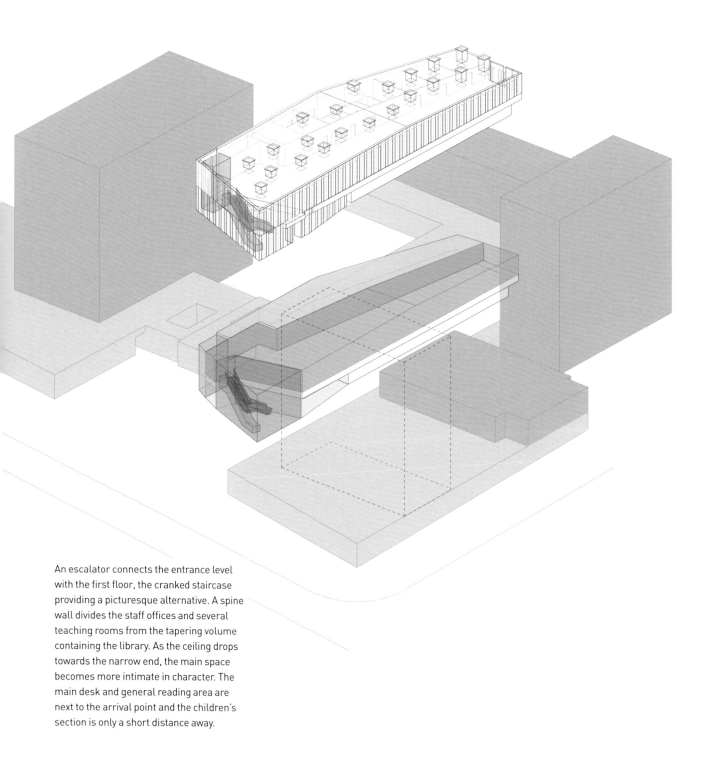

An escalator connects the entrance level
with the first floor, the cranked staircase
providing a picturesque alternative. A spine
wall divides the staff offices and several
teaching rooms from the tapering volume
containing the library. As the ceiling drops
towards the narrow end, the main space
becomes more intimate in character. The
main desk and general reading area are
next to the arrival point and the children's
section is only a short distance away.

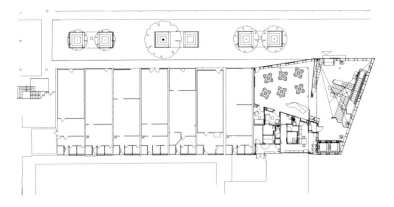

GROUND-FLOOR PLAN

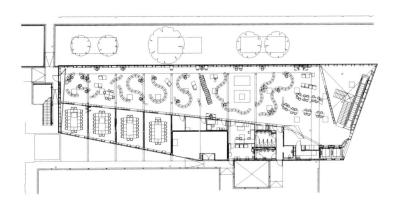

FIRST-FLOOR PLAN

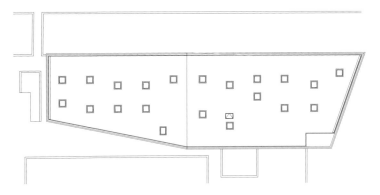

ROOF PLAN

1 Cafe and seating area
2 Children's library
3 Audio visual
4 Teen library
5 Adult library
6 Exhibition area
7 Open learning centre
8 Existing shop units

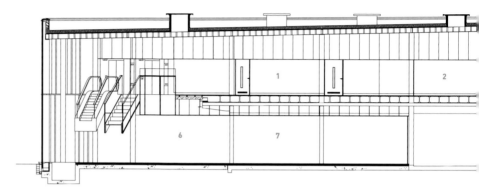

LONG SECTION

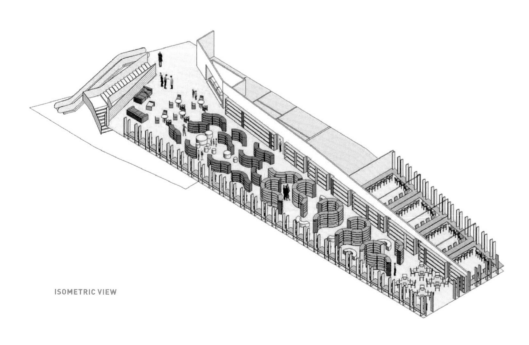

ISOMETRIC VIEW

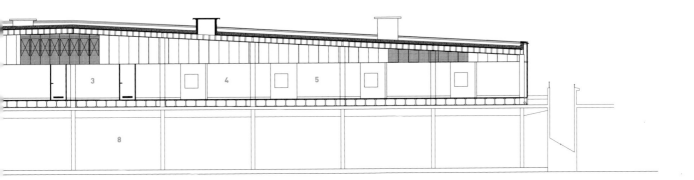

Tall Curvy Shelving
A system of flexible shelf units that can be used to make enclosed spaces within the larger space of the library.

Curved Shelving Unit
This has bookshelves on the outer face and a work surface on the inner face.

Exhibition Display Unit
Located in the entrance space, this is used to display any items of current interest.

Help Desk
The angled front allows for wheelchair users to move close to the desk.

Deck level provides a datum for the sectional organisation of the project. The position of the main library and the means of reaching it are immediately clear on entering the building. On the upper level, there are long views in each direction. To the north, the library space swells and then diminishes with an augmented perspective due to its tapering section. Looking across the entrance space, the statue of local shipbuilder Richard Green is visible on the far side of the East India Dock Road and, above his head, the skyline of Canary Wharf.

The use of glass on the south and east facades responds to the materiality of the adjacent shop fronts, as well as the requirements for the new building. The front facade is the most transparent, allowing the interior to be seen from the outside. On the east facade, the glass is sometimes backed by panels of insulation and this is where the bookshelves are located. The use of dark grey powder-coated aluminium panels on the north and west facades provides privacy for the housing and screens the library from the service area.

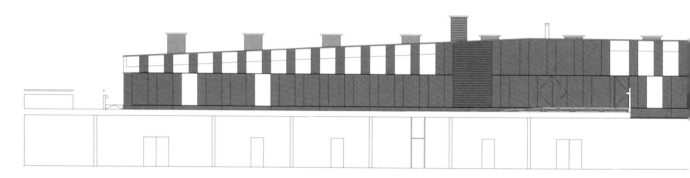

WEST ELEVATION

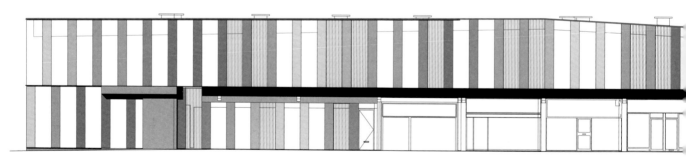

EAST ELEVATION

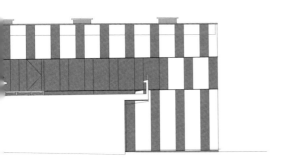

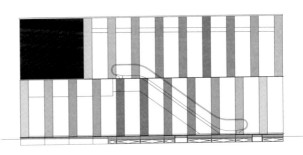

SOUTH ELEVATION

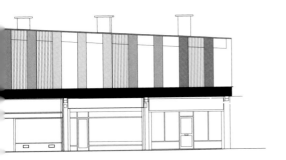

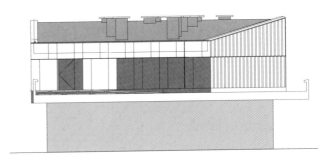

NORTH ELEVATION

SOUTH FACADE

EAST FACADE

NORTH FACADE

WEST FACADE

Above
Surfing area.

Left
Exhibition display unit,
surfing area behind.

Opposite
View from teaching space
into library.

10

TOWER HAMLETS

□ **Whitechapel**

LONDON

Idea Store Whitechapel
319 Whitechapel Road, London

Idea Store Whitechapel, 2001–2005

This project is located on the north side of Whitechapel Road where a wide pavement is occupied by a busy street market. Besides the traditional shop fronts, there are a number of more substantial buildings in the vicinity: Albion Yard, part of a former brewery, to the east and a mail sorting office and a hospital complex on the opposite side of the road. Reflecting its significance for the local community, the Idea Store takes its scale from these larger buildings. But its materiality is inspired by the nearby market stalls whose framed superstructures are draped in green and blue-striped sheets. A pedestrian passage, along the east side of the site, leads to the local supermarket.

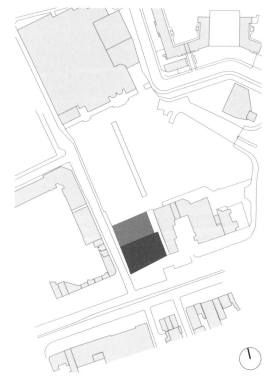

SITE PLAN

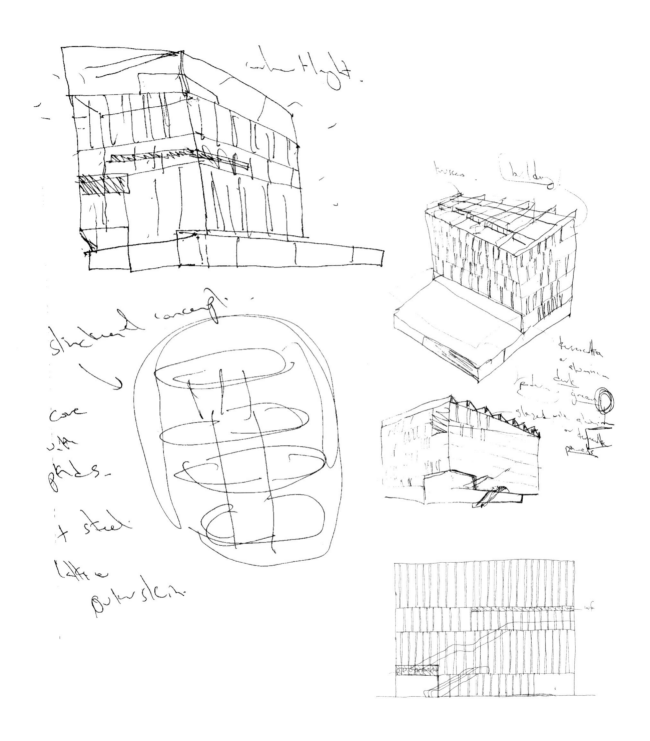

IDEA STORE WHITECHAPEL 183

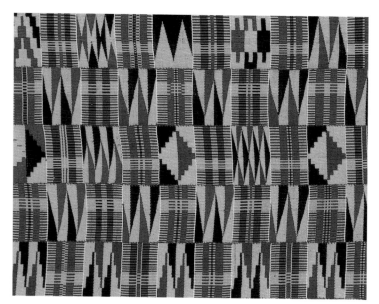

Textile, Ghana
A two-way grid with diagonal patterns.

The brief included a range of activities which have been layered together so that it is easy to move between them. This is reflected in the spatial organisation of the interior and in the selection of materials and how they are used. The laminated timber fins, which stiffen the external walls, support bookshelves, work surfaces and storage in a variety of positions throughout the building. Co-ordination between inside and outside is maintained by a loose grid whose lines of continuity are the horizontals of each floor and the structural steel blades visible in the continuous vertical lines on each facade.

Area Schedule

Adult Library 1010m²	
Circulation 560m²	
Classrooms 340m²	
Children's Library 330m²	
Ancillary 205m²	
Cafe 165m²	
IT / Surfing 150m²	
Dance Studio 140m²	
Staff Offices 125m²	
Audio Visual Library 110m²	
Creche 95m²	
Complementary Therapy 85m²	
Info / Exhibition 75m²	
Teen Library 50m²	

Total Area 3440m²

Materials

| Laminated green glass | Laminated blue glass | Laminated clear glass | Concrete | Perforated steel | Laminated veneer lumber | Wood fibre board | Spruce plywood | Red rubber flooring |

Site Concept

Empty box
Had the area of the site been developed to the height of the buildings on either side, this would have ignored the scale of the side street and would have dominated the site occupied by the supermarket.

Podium
The height of the back half of the building is dropped in order to create a platform which overlooks the supermarket car park. This provides a location for the dance studio and an alternative therapies space.

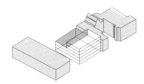

Deck
At the eastern side of the podium, there is an open deck which is accessible from the main building and the facilities at podium level. The position of this deck improves the lighting to the pedestrian passage.

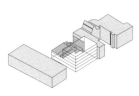

Angled front
To establish a presence on this busy thoroughfare, the western corner of the front facade is pulled forward by 3.3m. The projecting end is seen as a vertical banner from the west and the angled facade, incorporating an information screen, changes the perspective of the building when it is approached from the east.

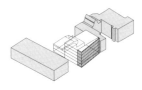

Entrance
The angled facade does not continue to the ground. The space which it protects becomes an entrance zone, with an escalator to the first floor and a ground floor entrance at opposite ends. There is also a protected entrance half-way along the pedestrian passage.

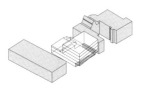

Roof
The building's plant rooms are located on the roof, on either side of the service core which connects all levels.

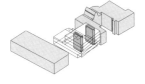

Context
In its form and organisation, the building has a strong relationship with its immediate surroundings and the wider context.

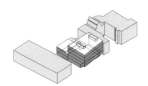

Facade system and assembly of volumes

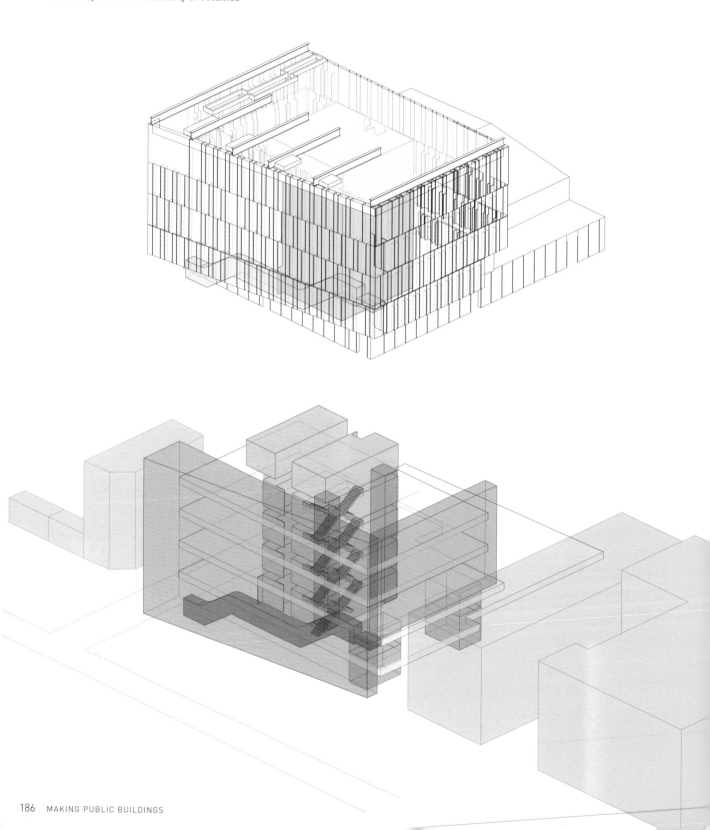

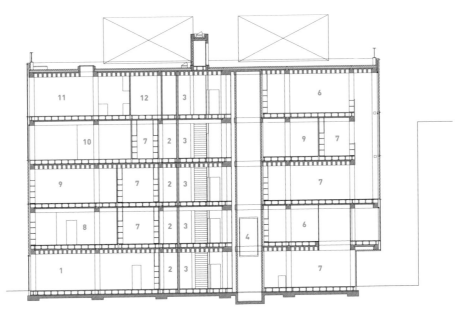

LONG SECTION

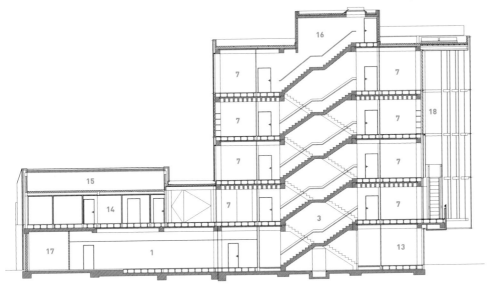

CROSS SECTION

1 Children's Library
2 Storage
3 Staircase
4 Lift
5 Entrance
6 Surfing space
7 Adult library
8 Creche
9 Classroom
10 Work room
11 Cafe
12 Cafe preparations
13 Escape lobby
14 Changing rooms
15 Plant
16 Roof Access
17 Server Room
18 Atrium

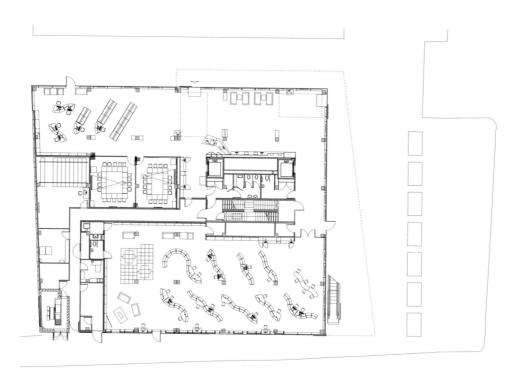

GROUND-FLOOR PLAN

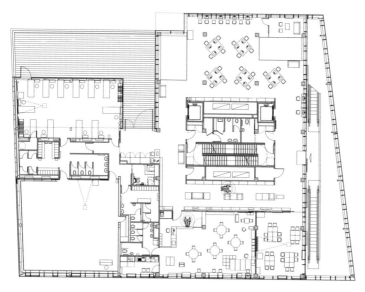

FIRST-FLOOR PLAN

This Idea Store can be seen as a single building or as a group of buildings. The first floor forms a *piano nobile* with an entrance located on the central axis. It connects the library facilities with the community spaces and both of these, via the open deck, to the space occupied by the supermarket. Together with the angling of the front facade, the geometry of the lower floors responds to the boundary conditions of the site and allows the remaining floors to ascend in a rectangular tower. On each level, an arcaded space loops around the bifurcated service core giving views of the interior and the surrounding area. The abstract qualities of the plans and section are complemented by the warmth of the timber fins, the rubber floor and the suspended lights. Without them, the interior would be more austere.

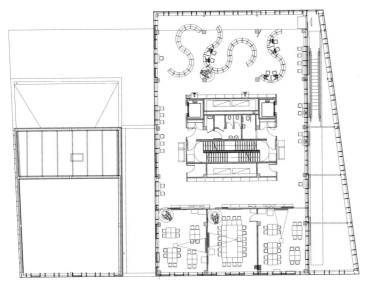

SECOND-FLOOR PLAN

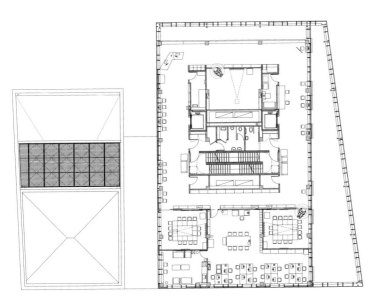

THIRD-FLOOR PLAN

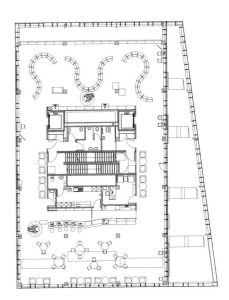

FOURTH-FLOOR PLAN

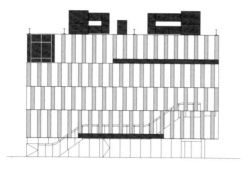

SOUTH ELEVATION

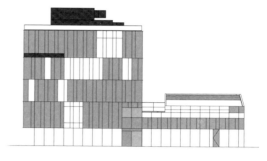

EAST ELEVATION

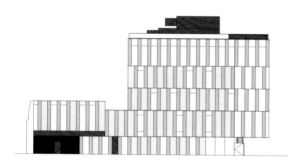

WEST ELEVATION

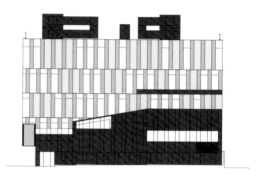

NORTH ELEVATION

The facades make use of the spatial fold demonstrated by the striped sheets that form the roofs of the nearby market stalls. This is especially clear in the case of the front facade, which is suspended from seven steel beams forming a cantilever in front of the main roof, and the east facade, which hangs from a cantilevered section of the main roof. The front facade is the most transparent and the east facade, with its aluminium panels reflecting light into the pedestrian passage, is the most solid. The lower section of the north elevation is directly comparable to the west facade of the Chrisp Street Idea Store.

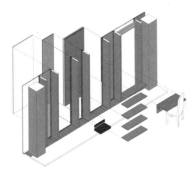

ELEMENTS OF FACADE

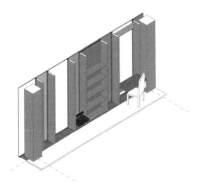

COMPLETED ASSEMBLY

Long Self-Issue Unit

The suspended front facade has two main functions: it shelters the escalator leading to the first and second floor entrances and it protects the inner facade from overheating in the summer. When the temperature in the enclosed void reaches a certain level, four vents open automatically in the roof. As the activities on the ground and first floors are closely linked, they are connected by two double-height spaces. The three floors above are linked by the triple-height space which is aligned with the position of the second floor entrance. The service core is divided by two interlocking stair-cases and the side walls of the service core and the inner face of the external walls are used to support bookshelves. At the end of several routes starting at street level, the cafe is lit by three rooflights and enjoys a fine view of Whitechapel Road and the skyline of the City of London.

Curvy Shelving
A system of flexible shelf units that can be used to make enclosed spaces within the larger space of the library.

Help Desk
The angled front allows for wheelchair users to move close to the desk.

Internet Bar and Servery

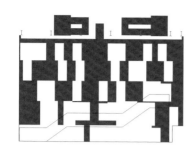

SOUTH FACADE

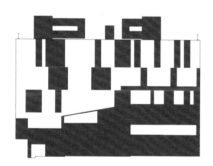

WEST FACADE

NORTH FACADE

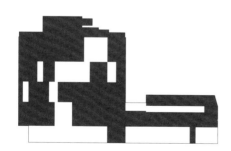

EAST FACADE

Right
Looking west from cafe.

Opposite
West facade seen from
Whitechapel Road.

Above
Pedestrian passage and east
facade. View from ground floor
entrance to audio visual library.

Left
Children's library.

Above
View from entrance
to street market.

Right
Escalator leading to first
and second floor entrances.
West facade with coloured
reflections.

Right
Detail of south facade
showing top of escalator.
Suspended atrium and
escalator.

Far right
Suspended atrium, view from
second floor looking west.

Below
Suspended atrium, looking
down from first floor.

Above
Adult library, gallery space.

Left
Adult library, door to
classroom. Staircase.

Opposite
Adult library, second floor
entrance space.

Above
Detail of south facade.
Classroom.

Right
Worktops and bookshelves
supported by north facade.

Above
View of cafe
showing rooflights.

Right
Looking west
from cafe.

Far Right
Cafe, servery and
surfing bar.

Left
Night view, north facade.

Below
Night view, south facade.

LEARNING FROM LAGOS: A DIALOGUE ON THE POETICS OF INFORMAL HABITATION

DAVID ADJAYE IN CONVERSATION WITH KODWO ESHUN

DAVID ADJAYE: Lets begin with a set of images of Islamic influenced cities in Mali (fig.1), then move through to cliff settlements (fig.2) and to those colonial settlements which have now become post-colonial. This is Dogon architecture, which completely blurs the act of understanding what architecture is (fig.3). These piles of rubble are actually doing something; they act as screens delineating privacy. There is an incredible informality, they look like a pile of nothing.

KODWO ESHUN: They look unformed. The act of intervention is hardly there, which actually means that it's a rather delicately managed arrangement.

DA: Exactly. It is an arrangement that is as designed as any other, because there is a purposeful hand there. But the condition has been understood and then amplified to deal with a social condition. There is a sense in using the economy of trees, as they are large enough to form a canopy, a shelter or rest area (fig.4). The traditional way of doing this is to erect straight columns but here there is an acceptance that it is the junction at the top that is relevant; this is what the local scenario demands that you do. What is interesting about how Islam dealt with North Africa, indeed most of Africa, is that it didn't impose an architectural ordering system. It implies a series of spaces in order to amplify the function that they serve. It implies gathering spaces to allow people to feel themselves as collectives, yet it still completely works within the language of the mud vernacular. Unlike a colonial condition, where a classical vernacular tries to adjust to the tropical while remaining essentially the same kind of architecture, here you have something which actually understands the condition of habitation and civilisation and allows the two to come together, to imbricate each other to form this architecture.

KE: Because of the nature of religion, you might assume that it would instantly hierarchise its relationship with the vernacular; it would instantly regard itself as a top down, aspirational model that the vernacular has to reach up and aspire to. Yet here you've described another relation altogether.

DA: It's different from Roman Catholic or Methodist churches in West Africa, which are wholesale replicas.

KE: In those instances the church functions as an ideological state apparatus in a way that resembles certain kinds of hospitals, schools or embassies. The verticality of the Catholic church not only insists on its superiority to the urban vernacular, it loudly demands a distinctive mode of genuflection from its congregation rather than investing in a horizontality that spreads out to participate in the lateral modes of everyday sociality.

DA: Let's now look at a place like Rwanda. People only associate it with the recent history of genocide; they don't actually have a physical image of it yet. Rwanda is a rural country, 90% of the population lives outside of urban settlements, and it is probably one of the most beautiful countries in the world in terms of climate, location and latitude (fig.5). Yet in its capital Kigali the Belgians, the colonial masters of the city, set up a festive modernist architecture that weaves its way through grand boulevards. Alongside this modernist master-planning there is an economic deprivation and also an opportunistic kind of negotiation. It gives rise to a layering that fills the gaps between the typological modernist grid and the sunlight pattern. You have a densification of the street plane that was not envisaged in original plans, which predicted that people would walk through arcades. What you find instead is a kind of densification, which in turn leads to a humanising of the architectural scale. You get a horizontal spread that is being choreographed by human activity, in front of the verticality of the architecture (fig.6). I think Whitechapel Road in East London does this beautifully, instinctively.

KE: Whitechapel Road is fascinating because there is a double register. A market on the pavement runs parallel to the shops — another form of market. Human traffic has to weave in between these lanes, so the street narrows even though the pavement is really wide.

DA: Its a massive pavement. You can liken it to the famous plaza in Barcelona.

KE: La Rambla.

DA: The Rambla in Barcelona has a fantastic linearity. It generates a diagram that makes no sense as a plan but that has a certain relevance to human interaction, — although there you have traffic weaving down the sides, and the Rambla suspended in the middle. It speaks of a real desire for this notion of linear human corridors of activity. At its most simplistic, that idea becomes the mall; a banal solution, because it is too abstracted and too desensitised from the wonderful range of human activity that can occur. When you look at Whitechapel Road, on the other hand, there is a layering that moves from the architecture to the market stall canopies and spreads beyond. It's a form of diffusion. Then you have an edge canopy, an overhang of the market on the other side that then contains this beautiful activity.

KE: It's some distance to walk between Whitechapel and Aldgate, which borders on London's financial district, the City. It allows for a dimension that the urban theorist Abdoumalique Simone identifies very well. He points to a condition which combines people working with others who inhabit space in a mode of informality

and potentiality. Simone writes that 'Public space is elaborated not only to re-confirm social ties or legitimate everyday practices and attitudes, but also to create the impression that certain social realities, alliances, loyalties and political and economic activities are taking place, regardless of whether or not they are taking place in actuality. Working assessments are made of potential opportunities and prevailing realities and a potential network of relations is maintained that need not be formalised in the present, but which exists in some imminent state for future mobilisation when necessary.' [1] I think the key phrase there is potential network.

DA: Absolutely, 'potential network' is the active phrase there. I think this is exactly what is misunderstood about the public realm and the way in which publicness occurs, which is fully demonstrated when you work in cities like this. Because by trying to use a code of formal publicness, you switch off that constant state of potentiality; that need people have to be near to that constant state of potential, and thereby to constitute it as a kind of active performance.

KE: Perhaps that potentiality is perceived as an imminent threat, as a possibility which can move in any number of directions, become potentially disruptive to a social fabric, and therefore must be coded immediately?

DA: Yes, yes. So it is aestheticised and that aestheticising becomes very monofunctional, which destroys any of the opportunity that is being created, that is being generated and being explored.

KE: You cannot plan for this publicness but maybe you can set up some initial parameters for it.

DA: You can initialise it in a way. It is almost like setting the stage for the activity by understanding the parameter of the activity. Once you have understood that, then you can begin to make a building which will start to imbricate itself. Only in this way can you explore potential new ways of making building choreographies and scenarios that actually engage very directly with general human activity.

KE: Let's have a look at something else.

DA: Let's go to Ghana. This is the coast (fig.7), just behind Nkrumah Park, Jamestown (fig.8). This is really looking down to the back lands of Makola (fig.9) and this is looking at the city library (fig.10), which is just by the national bank. I find this emblematic of a particularly fascinating moment, that between colonial leaving and the ambition of the new rhetoric of architecture, which Nkrumah is principally responsible for. It is based on this notion of trying to hijack modernism, to bend it to become a tropical modernism. That was precisely his agenda — to make a tropical modernity that spoke of a new language but actually engaged with the context of place in order to set up new scenarios. Now what is interesting is that the failure to curate the habitation of the city leads you to today's reality. It's a reality that is typologically fascinating, but absolutely against the grid. These incredible sheds fill up and then inhabit and densify the notion of the European downtown area. I think that in Africa, the Islamic world understood that it had to bring certain ideological structures, but that it also had to allow local specificity to co-opt them in order to have any chance of success, of being appropriate.

KE: What is at stake is modernisation: how to constitute a whole set of divergent collectivities into a nation that agrees on the narrative of modernisation. At full speed and with no turning back. How do you constitute that grandeur? In the wake of that project, in the niches, in the interstices of that implosion, you get the emergence of an informal illegal sector.

DA: In Soweto there is one such attempt to find ways of instituting informality into notions of formality. Instead of insisting on the need to do away with the ghetto, they have begun to ask what you might learn from the ghetto, what it tells you in terms of typology and layout so that the worst parts can be overturned while the positive aspect of proximity — and the kind of relationships that are being asked for — can somehow thrive. I am very much questioning the validity of imposing certain notions of modernity on the world.

KE: Two theorists, James Holsten and Arjun Appadurai, can speak to that scepticism. In 1996 they wrote that 'Modernist planning does not admit or develop productively the paradoxes of its imagined futures. Instead it attempts to be a plan without contradictions or conflict. It assumes a random domination of the future in which its total and totalising plan dissolves any conflict between these imagined and existing society in the enforced coherence of its order. This assumption is false and arrogant as it fails to include as its constituent element conflict, ambiguity and indeterminacy characteristic of actual social life.' [2]

DA: Modernity in this sense is not about reality but a utopian idea based on certain kinds of economic privileges. These privileges have to be there in perpetuity in order to allow for the repair, the maintenance, the kind of active infrastructure that …

KE: were never there to begin with. The implication of that condition might be what Lawrence Liang identifies as the state of illegality in cities like New Delhi, Sao Paolo and Lagos. He suggests that 'Recent research shows that an average of 40%, in some cases 70% of the population, of major cities live in illegal conditions. Furthermore, 70 to 95% of all new housing is built illegally and the primary reason for this state of illegality rises from the nature of land tenure forms in cities.

The twin tropes of ownership and title are clearly unable to account for the myriad ways in which people actually assert to claim on land and to the city more generally.'[3]

DA: In a way you could argue that the birth of building societies and the empowerment of the middle classes in the West eradicated that phenomenon, because it propelled the huge development culture that suddenly took hold in European cities. Previously, the middle classes had been tenants renting from landed gentry who would build according to their businesses. The recent changes have enabled what I call the first wave of developing culture.

KE: These practices never get going in the global south, not to the same extent and certainly not enough to underpin and to act as the engine for the kind of serial forms of occupation, ownership, building structure, habituation which constitute western modernity in the global north. The infrastructural drive is never there to begin with, so modernity in that sense is always delayed. Building is always put on hold while the infrastructure is instantiated. But that delay becomes interminable too. In the meantime you have a void which the multitudes inhabit. They cannot wait.

DA: They don't want to wait. They have to live their lives. They have to build, formulate habitable conditions which will make their lives work. But these are not desperate measures. A shantytown developed by a city planner becomes a linear prison. Yet a shantytown developed by people, is an agglomeration of networks and connections that interweave into each other and form bigger or smaller kinds of localities. Not in the way that we understand localities, in terms of squares and plazas. I think this is fascinating because we are talking about a co-dependency which allows survival to be much more easy. This is not insignificant, because the idea that somehow you will one day catch up with the West is a complete fallacy. I think conviviality is the underplayed

agent in this. Visiting most of these places, what became clear to me was that they required a different kind of looking. If you focus on the poverty and directly compare it with the situation here, you will be horrified. But if your eyes adjust from looking at comparisons to considering adaptation, then you see an urbanism that could be learned from. It doesn't occur top down, but sustains an entire community who would otherwise have fallen by the wayside as they waited for government to do something.

KE: Public space as space scripted by government does not exist, but neither does privatised space as scripted by corporations. So you have voids that are catastrophic at the same time as surpluses that animate human habitation, make it worth living and worth enjoying. It is difficult to point to this condition without validating it as a new model.

DA: One isn't actually saying: here is a much better pattern of social network and human habitation. What we are looking at here is not a singular theoretical paradigm of human habitation but multiple levels of human paradigm which are all equivalent. The model should no longer be an image of the world as a kind of singular project; it should be a series of equivalent systems, each with their own advantages and disadvantages. As an architect, or as an urbanist or a social thinker, one can work within all these paradigms. Now we move on to another example: Eritrea, where you have a fully applied colonial model — you make Rome in Africa. Asmaria resembles a section of Rome, completely designed within the kind of rationalist architecture of the time, so it is both futurist and rationalist.

KE: It looks like Sant Elia.

DA: It looks like a Sant Elia drawing built in Africa. This is a building for Fiat (fig. 11). Standing there one believes that the Italians were dreaming of flying back home; the efficiency of the industrial age becomes a metaphor for dreaming. But what is more interesting is how an African population suddenly appropriates this imposition and starts to use it as a structure to live their lives in. This is a Roman city thrown into an African country, but this is an African culture operating. Take the *passeggiata*, the southern Italian idea that you just spend the afternoon strolling, you browse, you gaze. This is very parallel to what Africans do, so there is a kind of similarity which is taken up; but in Africa it is not about families dressing up and looking at each other. The African *passeggiata* is about the energy of the city when the sun has gone down and everybody wants to convivially come together. I am completely fascinated by the palm trees that augment or distort the image of the futurist city (fig.12).

KE: It is a non-incongruous incongruity. So the Italians went further ...

DA: than the British, the French, the Dutch, the Germans, because they built a complete and functioning city, with its own infrastructure. The ultimate perversion was that they built it specifically for half a million Italians. The local Asmarians lived on the periphery in what was very much an apartheid system. The Asmarians worked in the city but left. In a way it was the first apartheid state. In the process, the Italians developed what none of the colonial predecessors had done, setting up a full infrastructure at huge expense to Mussolini, who was hell-bent on dominating that part of Africa. Nearly seventy or eighty years later, the Asmarians have this incredible city which they have now completely appropriated and made theirs.

KE: From Eritrea to?

DA: Ethiopia. This is a northern Ethiopian town, again a settlement town, which I really wanted to understand as a world heritage city with a North African architecture that is influenced by the Byzantine. This is a model of how the old architecture becomes a container for the kind of modernity that runs through it (figs. 13–14).

KE: And what are these yellow and blue containers?

DA: Containers seem to be very important in the area and obviously some manufacturer, probably Italian, is importing containers for water or fuel. This is a commodity that was bought and traded and recycled, because it is very valuable. So you have a lot of container architecture being assembled everywhere within the city walls, which are built of mud and brick and timber.

KE: And here?

DA: This is the idea of an overhang between the streets and balconies so that the public and private realms become really close (fig.15). On the street, you are literally on top of the balconies of people who are living above you, but the balconies also provide shade for the street. You get this very interesting density that I think is incredibly unusual. It has to do with the way in which the city as a ground plane has had to grow, and in which it has made itself three-dimensional by cross-weaving a second layer.

KE: Let me summarise our conversation so far. In the spaces of the social evacuated by socialist plan and exacerbated by uneven privatisation, the multitudes act for themselves without consultation, representation or delegation. Multiple habitations at horizontalizing levels densify the urban in response to specific needs. Part of your project is to understand this process in terms of a non-apocalyptic, non-developmental mode, that is neither about an older comparative idea of achieving parity but yet cannot be reduced to a set of simple survival strategies. You are proposing ways in which one might begin to understand some of the informal aesthetic choices being made here; choices that then create the possibilities for a conviviality in excess of desperation, such that it no longer becomes possible to read these networks as indexes of a dire economic situation. There is more at stake here that requires a particular kind of attentiveness in thinking about habitation.

DA: Yes, very much so. In looking at the Southern states, I am interested in trying to produce a non-hierarchical visioning of the urban environment. So that one no longer accepts an evolutionist idea of development, but instead explores a much more expansive and horizontal set of evolved states, working within those to really understand what is happening. Only then can one escape the tyranny of an architecture obsessed with aesthetics that are still derived from a Greek tradition. I think this critique is extremely important, because what we have now is an exhausted modernism applied as a hyperaesthetic.

KE: Let us move on to South Africa.

DA: This is in Soweto, in the Transvaal, in particular some of the Ndebele villages (fig.16). This is African suburbia, middle class black Africa, just outside Soweto (fig.20). These here are interstitial spaces between suburbia and Soweto, places where units have been built for storage and not for habitation (fig.s 18–19). I'm interested in the fact that a certain aesthetic is applied in a very specific way, as a form of selection process for appropriateness. When the memory of the original purpose or sign of this material is lost, and you use this material as found, you generate a different aesthetic. One tends to think that this material is about standardisation, which it is; but here it is not used in these terms. The material is resignified into a skin. What is really fascinating to me is how this material transformation occurs through a process that seems unaviodable but is utterly subtle. I'm fascinated by the ways that vernacular cultures appropriate materials to bring them into a purpose which fits the cultural frame, rather than the other way round.

KE: Standardisation has been melted into a skin that becomes appropriate to the conditions of its ...

DA: its locale, its geography, its cultural context, its environmental context. It is a customization of standardisation that is really powerful.

KE: The precision and exactitude of that customization is where the aesthetics lie, in the set of aesthetic preferences which are partly determined by the material and partially by the preferences of the makers. It is their idea of what customization is that allows the roof to bend at a certain point in order ...

DA: To drain the water.

KE: The stones at the bottom of the house?

DA: To deal with protecting the base of the building, elevating it off the ground.

KE: And these cracks?

DA: Ventilators probably, allowing the building to breathe. Because they are not trying to make hermetic structures. These are almost tent-like.

KE: Yes, a tent made out of metal. The windows ...

DA: are flaps that just, you know, hinge out.

KE: They're rusting.

DA: Yes, its rusted metal, but the composition is amazing. It is corrugated and then weighted on the top. Now if you looked at a nomadic group, you would see a similar architecture to that made out of skins.

KE: How long has it taken you to come to this understanding of these kinds of vernacular appropriation?

DA: I think I have been conscious of it for about ten years. After I finished my education, I refocused my intention to re-look with a new set of eyes at conditions that I already knew. I reprogrammed myself to no longer look at these things as conditions of crises. Once it happened, it opened up a whole new way of working.

KE: Actuality then begins to pressurise language and to exceed the concepts of value and the capacity of judgement. At that point both are suspended and then re-emerge, recalibrated along a plane of horizontality.

DA: Yes. The early work that I did was all about a resignification of materiality. The response was, gosh, you know these are unusual materials that are being deployed within the work. Now I can see that those pieces allowed for a way of questioning the performance of materiality within particular notions of assemblage.

KE: What is going on at this point?

DA: This is a Ndebele village that appears to be built in a completely vernacular tradition, but you realise that in fact this is a very contemporary condition. What's amazing about the Ndebele is that after practically being wiped out, they have remade their culture anew. So what you're looking at is the appropriation of modernism, completely recontextualised into a culturally appropriate frame. You can have two kinds of assemblages: on the one hand there is pastiche, which is a kind of romantic throwback to something, reapplied but very thinly. On the other you can have an agglomeration of different systems which form yet another system, one that is very

specifically related to its own context. The second model is very much at play here. The homes are laced by this network of lines and walls that turn spaces into very defined thresholds and courtyards. The suburban model hinges on the singular house but with the Ndebele, the singular house is in relationship to the next house. Its connectivity arises from a network of walls that somehow stitches all the huts together to form a community.

KE: What have we got next? Brazil?

DA: These are shots of some of the favelas above Rio (fig.s 21–22). I'm struck by this notion of hill towns and cliff towns as a mat of civilisation, a network that sits on a landscape. This is closer in. You've got this house that has been built by construction workers, who are building creatively because they cannot afford to dig out the landscape and place boxes within it. So they are just naturally adapting to the flow and contour of the landscape, which gives rise to a very unique kind of pattern. When you go up into the favelas, their very specific identity is striking. They are very responsive to context, as opposed to the way that downtown buildings are built in the applied grid of an abstracted cityscape.

KE: And then to India.

DA: Today there is an international style of tower building in Bangalore and Bombay, but there is also an urge for specificity which bends the tower into a very localised condition. The inappropriateness of the colonial city is made appropriate by the notion of the lightweight arcade. It is an accretion that applies itself to this architecture in order to animate a certain kind of social life that needs to exist on a ground plane. It creates awnings that stretch full width across the street and that you can walk beneath.

KE: The appropriateness of human scale as a graduation

of levels relates to an idea expressed by Walter Benjamin in his essay on Naples. He suggests that 'porosity is the inexhaustible law of life in this city, reappearing everywhere, building an action, interpenetrating the courtyards, arcades and stairways to become a theatre of new unforeseen constellations. The stamp of the definitive is avoided'. [4] How might that insufficiency and incompleteness relate to an immersive pirate culture?

DA: What is interesting to me is not so much the pirating, but the fact that another technology is inflected and then amplified as an appropriate way of getting information to people extremely quickly. It's similar to the way that radios provided an extraordinary means of communication when they were first introduced.

KE: At a certain point pirate media becomes part of the urban fabric itself. There is a way in which pirate culture is co-dependent with the informal habitations and patterns of accretion that we have been talking about. It is not a question of incongruity, alienation or disjunction. Monica Narula of Raqs Media Collective develops this idea. She writes about the notion of seepage in relation to those networks that fall outside of official maps and official plans. She suggests that people have insider knowledge of today's networked world and of how this network makes itself known in our consciousness. 'By seepage we mean the action of many currents of fluid material leeching onto a stable structure and entering and spreading through it by way of pores, until it becomes a part of the structure … at the same time continues to act on its core, to gradually disaggregate its solidity, to crumble it over time with moisture. Initially the process is invisible and then it slowly starts causing mould and settles into a disfiguration and this produces an anxiety about the strength and the durability of the structure. The implication of this is that seepage in and of itself is not an alternative. It needs the structure to become what it is, but it creates new conditions in which

structures become fragile and are rendered difficult to sustain, it enables the play of an alternative imagination. In a networked world there are many acts of seepage: they destabilise the structure without making any claims. The trespasser alters the border by crossing it, rendering it meaningless and yet making it present everywhere, even in the heart of the capital city, so that every citizen becomes a suspect alien and the compact of citizenship which sustains the state is quietly eroded. The pirate renders impossible the difference between the authorised and the unauthorised copy, spreading information and culture and devaluing intellectual property at the same time. Seepage complicates the norm by inducing invisible structural change that accumulates over time.' [5]

DA: A good point at which to stop perhaps. Its a fascinating analogy in terms of fluid dynamics. A similar notion could be applied to the way that vines work with walls in a symbiotic way; they start to destabilise the wall and eventually the two cohabit. And co-dependency becomes a requirement of this cohabitation.

Notes

1. *Lawrence Liang, Porous Legalities and Avenues of Participation, Sarai READER 05: BARE ACTS (eds) Monica Narula, Shuddhabrata Sengupta, Jeebesh Bagchi + Geert Lovink, (Delhi: The Sarai Programme, Centre for the Study of Developing Societies, 2005) p. 6.*

2. *James Holsten and Arjun Appadurai, Cities and Citizenship in Public Culture, Vol 8, No 2, Winter 1996. Cited in L.Liang, op. cit, p. 7.*

3. *Walter Benjamin and Asja Lacis, Naples. Reflections: Essays, Aphorisms, Autobiographical writings, ed. Peter Demetz (New York: Shocken Books Inc, 1986), p. 166–7.*

4. *Raqs Media Collective, X-Notes on Practice: Stubborn Structures and Insistent Seepage in a Networked World, forthcoming, Immaterial Labour: Work, Research, Art (eds) Marina Vishmidt and Melanie Giligan (London/New York: Black Dog Publishing, 2005). Also available at www.raqsmediacollective.net/textsl.html*

5. *Abdoumaliq Simone, Globalizing Urban Economies, Documenta 11 Platform 5: Exhibition Catalogue (Kassel: Hatje Cantz Publishers, 2002) p. 118.*

1   Great mosque of Djene   2   Shelter area in Dogon village   3   Bereli village in Dogon

4   Segou village shop   5   Countryside outside Kigali   6   High street, Kigali

7   View towards sea, Jamestown   8   Nkrumah gardens, Jamestown   9   Area behind Makola market, Jamestown

10   City library, Jamestown   11   Fiat building, Asmara   12   Passeggiata, Asmara

13

14

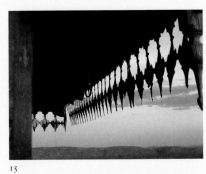

15

16

17

18

19

20

21

22

23

24

13 Residential street, Harer

14 Public street, Harer

15 Rooftop detail structure, Harer

16 Ndebele housing, Transvaal

17 View of Soweto

18 Detail of housing, Soweto

19 Detail of shop, Soweto

20 Housing in a Soweto suburb

21 Favela outside Rio de Janeiro

22 Main highstreet in a Rio de Janeiro favella

23 Shopping / residential area, Delhi

24 Street scene, Delhi

Biographical Notes

David Adjaye

Born in Dar–Es–Salaam, Tanzania to
Ghanaian parents on 22 September, 1966.
Lives in Middle East and Africa, 1966–1978.

Moves to London, UK, 1979. Attends Middlesex University
and receives a Diploma in Art and Design, 1985–1986.

Works in the offices of Chassay Architects, London, 1988–1990.

Attends Southbank University and receives
BA Hons Architecture RIBA Part I. Writes dissertation
on "Shibam, city in the desert, Yemen", 1989–1990.

Wins First Prize Bronze Medal from
Royal Institute of British Architects, 1990.

Works in the offices of David Chipperfield Architects,
London, 1991.

Works in the offices of Eduardo Souto de Moura Architects,
Portugal, 1991.

Attends Royal College of Art and receives
MA Architecture RIBA Part II. Writes dissertation
on "Sacred place and tea ceremony in Japan", 1991–1993.

Teaches at South Bank University from 1993–2002.

Starts architectural practice with William Russell in 1994.

Receives his RIBA Part III,
and becomes ARB registered in 1997.

Teaches at Royal College of Art from 1998–2002.

Reforms his practice as Adjaye/Associates, 2000.

Presents *Dreamspaces* series on modern architecture
for BBC: Series I, 2002; Series II, 2003.

Interviews Oscar Neimeyer in Brazil for BBC Radio 4, 2004.

Teaches at Architectural Association from 2003–2005.

Presents *Building Africa: The Architecture
of a Continent*, 2005 for BBC.

Interviews Charles Correa in India for BBC Radio 4, 2005.

Teaches at University of Pennsylvania 2006.

Selected Lectures

Harvard's Graduate School of Design, Cambridge, MA, 2001

University of Hanover, Germany, 2001

Universidad de Luisdad in Lisbon, Portugal, 2001

Cornell University, Ithaca, NY, 2002

Cambridge University, Cambridge, UK, 2002

Yale Univeristy, New Haven, CT, 2003

Art Center College of Design, Los Angeles, CA, 2003

Tate, Liverpool, UK, 2003

Royal College of Art, London, UK, 2004

Norsk Forum, Oslo, Norway, 2004

CCAC, San Francisco, CA, 2004

Univeristy of California-Berkeley, CA, 2004

Royal Academy, London, UK, 2004

Syracuse University, Syracuse, NY, 2005

University of Buffalo, Buffalo, NY, 2005

Illinois Institute of Technology Chicago, IL, 2005

Art Institute of Chicago, Chicago, IL, 2005

Urban Center, New York, NY, 2005

Rice Design Alliance, Houston, TX, 2005

Tate Britain, London, 2005

Selected Exhibitions / Recognition

Outside/In: London Architecture,
Architeckturforum, Innsbruck, Austria, 2000

Space Invaders, British Council, 2001

Next, Venice Biennale of Architecture, 2002

World Architecture Awards,
Best European House, Elektra House, 2002

Sâo Paulo Bienal, Brazil, 2003

Advisor to the LDA, Thames Gateway
Design Panel, 2003–2005

Metamorph, Venice Biennale
of Architecture, 2004

Recent Work of Emerging Architects,
GA Gallery, Tokyo, Japan, 2004

Idea Store Chrisp Street, RIBA Building Award, 2005

Contributors' Biographies

Peter Allison has curated exhibitions on contemporary Austrian architecture and new architecture from London. He contributes to a number of international publications and teaches in London. He recently edited *David Adjaye Houses*, Thames & Hudson, London 2005.

Okwui Enwezor is Dean of Academic Affairs at San Francisco Art Institute. He was the artistic director of Documenta 11 and the 2nd Johannesburg Biennial. He has served as visiting professor in art history at the University of Pittsburgh and Columbia University. He is currently the artistic director of the 2nd Biennial of Contemporary Art Seville.

Kodwo Eshun is author of *More Brilliant Than the Sun: Adventures in Sonic Fiction*. He has lectured and published widely on notions of futurity and archival practice. He is Course Leader of the MA in Aural and Visual Cultures at Goldsmiths College and is a founding member of the artists group *The Otolith Group*, whose work will be appearing at the 3rd Tate Triennale in March 2006.

Nikolaus Hirsch is joint founder of the practise Wandel, Lorch and Hirsch in Saarbrucken. He is the architect of the Dresden Synagogue and more recently the Hinzert Document Centre, Germany. He contributes to international architecture journals and publications.

Saskia Sassen teaches at the University of Chicago and London School of Economics. She is the author most recently of *Territory, Authority and Rights: From Medieval to Global Assemblages*, Princeton University Press, 2006 and contributor to major international publications.

Adjaye/Associates 2000–05

David Adjaye
Elizabeth Acquah
Sarah Adams
Doreen Adengo
Samson Adjei
Christopher Adjei
Rachel Adu
Yahya Ali
Rashid Ali
Ixone Altube
Alice Asafu–Adjaye
Angelita Alves Alfieri
Montunrayo Badu
Larissa Bailey
Anuschka Bayer
Yohannes Bereket
Christina Bianchi
Jennifer Boheim
Justin Bolton
Hannah Booth
Johanna Borkhamm
James Branch
Miranda Buck
James Carrigan
Josh Carver
Tannith Cattermole
Juanita Cheung
Kimiko Cho
Stijn Cockx
Bergendy Cooke
Achille Corradin
Mariana Vasco Costa
Charlotte Cumlin
Nikolai Delvendahl
Dieter De Vos
Corrina Donegan
Bertil Donker
Mansour El–Khawad
Cornelia Fischer-Ekhorn
Joseph Franchina
Soyingbe Gandonu
Robert Gay
Fawzia Ghafoor
Jessica Grainger
Shizuka Haiu
Emiko Hayakawa

Andrew Heid
Vinnie Hewett
Carolin Hinne
Juila Hochquesand
Wen Hui Foo
Sara Islam
Rebecca Jacoby
Ramona Jeuschenak
Martin Kaefer
Ruth Kedar
Ahmed Khouja
Haremi Kudo
Sindiso Khumalo
Minseok Kim
Andrea Krutzik
Aimee Lau
Rob Lowe
Josephine Macpherson
David Mah
Davide Marelli
Karoline Markus
Beza Nchong Mbeboh
Edward McCann
Sean McMahon
Yuko Minamide
Asako Mogi
John Moran
Julia Mueller
Sarah Murfin
Matias Musacchio
Alexandros Mykoniatis
Jennifer Newsom
Nadine Oerhrli
Sang Hoon Oh
Yetunde Olaiya
Elizabeth Odame–Yirenkyi
Cherrie Ouerghi
Kwanjoo Park
Avni Patel
Ana Rita Pereira da Silva
Rodrigues
Miriam Quansah
Alberto Sabata
Daniel Serafimovski
Beatrice Sampong
Bodo Schumacher

Fiona Scott
Jason Scoot
Alison Shean
Sebastian Spengler
Jonathan Steiner
Kofi Tamakloe
Craig Tan
Tsuyoshi Tane
Go Tashiro
Lucy Tilley
Paul La Tourelle
Jan Tupek
Matus Vallo
Victoria Von Knorring
Claudia Wess
Trevor Wilson
Karen Wong
Miriam Zuurbia

Current Staff
Former Staff

Credits

Book Concept
Adjaye/Associates

Graphic Design and Production Team
Hannah Booth, James Branch, Karen Wong

Photography
David Adjaye: *pp. 24, 60, 216–217*

Verity Allison: *pp. 195, 196 top left, 197 bottom right, 199 top, 202 top & bottom left, 204 bottom left, 205 left & right, 212 top & bottom left, 223 hardback, 224 softback*

Hannah Booth: *pp. 169, 171, 174, 177 left, 193, 194, 199 bottom, 200 middle*

Camerafoto Arte, Venezia: *pp. 88, 96–105*

Lyndon Douglas: *pp. 70, 125, 158, 172, 206, 207*

Tim Soar: *pp. 20, 22, 29, 30, 31, 32 bottom right, 33, 34, 35, 36–43, 173, 175, 176, 177 right, 178, 191, 194, 198 top, 201, 203, 204 right, 205 top, 212 right, 213*

Edmund Sumner: *pp. 196 top right & bottom, 198 bottom left & right, 200 top, 202 right, 204 top left*

Other Photos
p. 4: Cornelia Fischer-Ekhorn; *p. 19:* Peter Allison; *p. 22:* The Nobel Foundation; *p. 32 right:* Nils Petter Dale; *p. 32 top left:* Nikolai Delvendahl; *p. 46 right:* Angus Mill; *p. 90 right:* Elfie Semotan; *pp. 106, 118-119:* Mansour El-Khawad; *p. 108:* The Stephen Lawrence Charitable Trust; *p. 132:* The Bernie Grant Trust; *p. 146:* Dieter De Vos; *pp. 179, 180:* Sean McMahon; *pp. 197 bottom left, 200 bottom:* James Branch; *p. 197:* Karen Wong

Site, Material and Model Shots
(unless otherwise noted): Hannah Booth and James Branch

Illustrations
Studio Toni Yli-Suvanto
pp. 55, 67, 68–69, 74, 85, 140, 141, 153, 156–157

Images of Artifacts
p. 48: Paul Macapia, Seattle Art Museum, Gift of Katherine White and the Boeing Company
pp. 78, 92, 162, 184: Archives musée Dapper and Hughes Dubois
p. 110: The National Museum of Accra, Archives musée Dapper and Hughes Dubois
pp. 134, 148: Lynton Gardiner, American Museum of Natural History
p. 139: Hutchison Picture Library

Printers
EBS, Verona, Italy

Published on occasion of the exhibition

DAVID ADJAYE
MAKING PUBLIC BUILDINGS

Whitechapel Gallery, London
January 24th – March 26th, 2006

Netherlands Architecture Institute, Maastricht
Autumn 2006

The Studio Museum in Harlem, New York
Spring 2007

Museum of Contemporary Art, Denver
Autumn 2007

Arario Gallery, Beijing
Winter 2007

Curated by Andrea Tarsia
Organised by Chris Aldgate and Candy Stobbs
with additional support from Abi Barber

First published in the United Kingdom in 2006 by Thames & Hudson Ltd,
181A High Holborn, London WC1V 7QX

www.thamesandhudson.com

First paperback edition 2006

British Library Cataloguing-in-Publication Data
A catalogue record for this book is available from the British Library

ISBN-13: 978-0-500-28648-7

ISBN-10: 0-500-28648-5

Printed and bound in Italy